THE CANONICO-JURIDICAL STATUS OF A COMMUNIST

The writing of this dissertation was conducted under the direction of the Rev. John Rogg Schmidt, A.B., J.C.D., LL.B., as the major professor, and was approved by the Rev. Frederick R. McManus, A.B., J.C.D., and the Rev. John J. McGrath, A.B., LL.B., J.C.D., as readers.

THE CATHOLIC UNIVERSITY OF AMERICA
CANON LAW STUDIES
No. 400

The Canonico-Juridical Status of a Communist

A DISSERTATION

SUBMITTED TO THE FACULTY OF THE SCHOOL OF CANON LAW OF THE CATHOLIC UNIVERSITY OF AMERICA IN PARTIAL FULFILLMENT OF THE REQUIREMENTS FOR THE DEGREE OF DOCTOR OF CANON LAW

BY THE
REV. RICHARD J. MURPHY, O.M.I., S.T.L., J.C.L.
PRIEST OF THE EASTERN PROVINCE
OF THE CONGREGATION OF THE OBLATES OF MARY IMMACULATE

THE CATHOLIC UNIVERSITY OF AMERICA PRESS
WASHINGTON, D. C.
1959

IMPRIMI POTEST:

Raymund J. Hunt, O.M.I., Ph.D.

Superior Provincialis

Bostonii, die 29 Novembris, 1958

NIHIL OBSTAT:

John Rogg Schmidt, A.B., J.C.D., LL.B

Censor Deputatus

IMPRIMATUR:

Patrick A. O'Boyle

Archiepiscopus Washingtonensis

Washingtonii, D. C., die 2 Decembris, 1958

Murray and Heister, Inc.
Washington, D. C.

Printed by
Times and News Publishing Co.
Gettysburg, Pa., U.S.A.

To My Mother
and Father

FOREWORD

Karl Marx opened his famous *Communist Manifesto* by declaring, "A Spectre is haunting Europe—the spectre of Communism."[1] The *Manifesto* was published in 1848. Today, a little more than a hundred years later, that same spectre is haunting the whole of the civilized world. At present practically every country has a Communist Party, with the result that the over-all membership runs into the millions. Moreover, in addition to actual Party members, there are countless other non-Party Communists, or as they are called in this country, "Communist sympathizers," who daily assist in spreading the errors of Communism and widening its sphere of activity and influence.

It cannot be denied that not a few Catholics have succumbed to the allurements of Communism, despite the fact that the Holy See has on numerous occasions solemnly warned the faithful not to associate themselves with this movement. Some openly profess the errors of Communism; some merely join the Communist Party; while still others in some way show favor to the movement. The purpose of this dissertation is to determine the canonico-juridical status of such persons. The writer feels justified in referring to all three as Communists, since the Holy Office in its *Declaratio De Communistarum Matrimonii Celebratione,*[2] uses the term "Communist" in this wide sense; that is, as embracing those who profess the errors of Communism, those who join the Party, and those who show favor to the movement.

The first part of the dissertation is divided into two chapters. The first chapter presents a brief history of modern Communism, together with an examination of the structure and function of the Communist Party, its strategy and tactics. The writer feels that this general study of Communism will be helpful in determining

[1] *Communist Manifesto* (Chicago: Henry Regnery Co., 1949), p. 7.

[2] S.S.C.S. Off., declar., 11 Aug., 1949—*Acta Apostolicae Sedis, Commentarium Officiale* (Romae, 1909—), XXXXI (1949), 427 (hereafter cited as *AAS*).

the legal position of those who associate themselves with the movement. The second chapter sets forth the numerous condemnations of Communism made by the Holy See over the course of the past one hundred years.

The second part of the dissertation is similarly divided into two chapters. The first determines the canonico-juridical positions of the various categories of Communists just mentioned, while the second chapter of the second part focuses attention on some practical problems.

The writer is grateful to his Provincial, the Very Reverend Raymond J. Hunt, O.M.I., Ph.D., for the opportunity to pursue advance studies in Canon Law; and to the Reverend John Rogg Schmidt, A.B., J.C.D., LL.B., for the time and effort which he so generously gave in directing this dissertation. The writer also wishes to thank the members of the Faculty of the School of Canon Law for their counsel and direction.

TABLE OF CONTENTS

TABLE OF CONTENTS (Continued)

PART II

Canonical Commentary

TABLE OF CONTENTS (Continued)

PART I

Historical Survey of Communism

CHAPTER I

General History and Structure of the Communist Party

INTRODUCTION

The ultimate purpose of this work is to determine the canonico-juridical status of a Catholic who in one way or another becomes affiliated with the Communist movement. To accomplish this task it is essential to have some general knowledge of Communism—its history, its tactics, and the structure of the Communist Party.

ARTICLE 1. THE HISTORICAL DEVELOPMENT OF COMMUNISM

Section I. Remote Preparations

It is true that much of the success of the Communist movement can be attributed to its finely constructed organization, its rigid party discipline, its clear-cut objectives and the zeal of its members in pursuing those objectives, to say nothing of its ruthless brutality. However, the society which produced and so readily accepted this most pernicious philosophy must be taken into account. It must be remembered that the moral and spiritual defenses of the nineteenth century—the century in which Communism was activated—were at a point of collapse, having been rifled and softened by the combined attacks of liberalism, rationalism and atheism. In short, the moral fiber of the nineteenth century was such that it fell easy prey to the Communist onslaught, as has the twentieth century.

However, the decadence was not entirely the fault of the nineteenth century. Rather, it was for the most part a heritage from former times. McFadden in his splendid work, *The Philosophy of Communism,* traces in a logical fashion the gradual breakdown of society.[1] The liberalism, he notes, which was so characteristic

[1] *The Philosophy of Communism* (New York: Benziger Bros., Inc., 1939), pp. 3-7.

of the nineteenth century had its origins in the Renaissance when the appetites were released from the restraints which formerly made man their master. All too soon this spirit of liberalism was applied to the moral actions of man, and gradually the existence of an objective law which man's actions must conform to was eliminated.

In time liberalism found its expression in the Protestant revolt of the sixteenth century. Authority in religion was refused recognition and each man was given liberty to interpret Scripture as he pleased. Having taught man that there was no authority which should regulate his personal life, it was only natural that in time he would come to disregard the authority which governs his country. Thus arose political liberalism, expounded by such men as Rousseau, Hobbes, and the Encyclopedists.

"Finally," McFadden concludes, "with the coming of the machine age and the birth of the Industrial Revolution, the spirit of liberalism began to permeate the only remaining phase of human activity —the economic life of man."[2]

Adam Smith, one of the leading economic liberals of the eighteenth century, contributed greatly to the creation of still another form of liberalism, namely, individualism. He contended that each man knows best how to make himself rich, and therefore man should not be held down by regulations. This "age of enlightened self-interest," as it is often called, demanded the abolition of government restrictions on industry, and called for the abolishment of unions so that the employee might enter into private agreements with the employer. Finally, the individualists maintained that the state should act merely as a policeman to prevent the commission of crimes. Intellectually, the individualists championed freedom of thought, extolled the natural sciences and technology, and treated religion as a private affair of the individual conscience. It was every man for himself. Speaking of this period, Carlton J. Hayes says, "The golden rule and the command to love one's neighbor appeared now as pretty sentiments which it would be folly to practice."[3]

---

[2] *Ibid.*, p. 5.

[3] *A Political and Social History of Modern Europe* (2 vols., New York: Macmillan Co., 1918), II, 84.

From liberal individualism, the next step was Socialism and then Communism. It seems quite probable that in a certain sense the latter two were reactions to the former. To be sure the early Socialists adopted many of the principles of liberalism and rejected others. Paradoxically, they continued the liberal doctrine even while bitterly fighting against it.

Before concluding this section on the prelude to Communism, it is well to recall that both atheism and rationalism were integrally connected with the later developments of liberalism. Leo XIII in the introductory section of his encyclical on Socialism, Communism and Nihilism (*Quod Apostolici*) outlines the historical background to the development of these philosophies. In so doing he clearly demonstrates the disastrous effects of atheism and rationalism.[4] He recalls that because of the false doctrines of rationalism, governments were organized without God. Men were taught that public authority did not originate with God, but arose from the masses of the people. Slowly, he notes, the Author of Mankind was forced to withdraw from the scheme of studies at universities, colleges and high schools, as well as from daily life. At last, men lost sight of a future life with its rewards and punishments and focused their attention on this life.[5]

By the nineteenth century, because of liberalism, rationalism and atheism, many had lost their faith in God, and the necessary restraints of religion and morality were weakened or entirely removed. At the same time the Industrial Revolution was profoundly altering the course of civilization. Thousands of men were out of work. Homes and communities were uprooted. Poverty and misery were commonplace. Due to the competition for work, men were forced to labor long hours each day for meager wages. Women and children were obliged to seek employment in factories and mines where little attention was given to health or safety. Liberal individualism was in action.

---

[4] Leo XIII, encycl. *Quod Apostolici*, 28 Dec., 1878—*Codicis Iuris Canonici Fontes*, cura Emi. Petri Card. Gasparri editi (9 vols., Romae postea Civitate Vaticana: Typis Polyglottis Vaticanis, 1923-1939), III, n. 576 (hereafter cited as *Fontes*).

[5] *Encycl. cit.*, p. 126; cf. also Pius XI, encycl. *Divini Redemptoris*, 19 March, 1937—*AAS*, XXIX (1937), 73.

In the midst of such suffering, a society adrift from God and His Eternal Law, produced and readily accepted atheistic Communism.

Section II. Marxian Socialism

The early 1880's witnessed several attempts at the establishment of Socialist societies by such men as Owen, Fournier, Blanc, Proudhon, and Bakunin. Although these early movements—frequently styled "Utopian Socialism"—failed, they were instrumental in the formation of the later Marxian style of Socialism, or Communism. This form of Socialism—"Marxian Socialism"—drew its name from its chief designer, Karl Marx.

Kark Marx (1818-1883) attended the Universities of Bonn, Berlin, and Jena, receiving a degree of Doctor of Philosophy from the latter in 1841. A year after receiving his degree, he took an assignment writing for a radical paper in Cologne, *Rheinische Zeitung*. The industrious Marx rose to the position of editor in a short time, but the government soon forced the paper to close down because of its radical policies. It moved to Paris where it operated for only a short time.

Marx remained in Paris. There he came in contact with Proudhon, Blanc, Bakunin and a number of other Socialists. Proudhon, for some time, had been trying to apply the dialectics of Hegel to the social problems of the times. Because of his shallow knowledge of Hegel, his efforts proved unsatisfactory. Marx, on the other hand, since he had studied at the University of Berlin, the stronghold of Hegelianism, had a thorough knowledge of the philosophy. He eventually undertook and completed what Proudhon had failed to do. While in Paris he also spent considerable time with Bakunin and other Russian revolutionaries. McFadden observes that such contacts naturally had an effect on Marx and probably deepened the revolutionary spirit in his mind.[6]

In 1845 Marx moved to Brussels where he remained for three years, organizing workers' clubs and agitating for political democracy. While in Brussels, in collaboration with Frederick Engels, he produced the famous *Communist Manifesto*, in 1848. He chose

[6] McFadden, *The Philosophy of Communism*, p. 19.

the word "Communist" to distinguish this program from the program of the Utopian Socialists. The little pamphlet, a statement of principles for the workers' clubs, passed almost unnoticed at the time. Eventually, however, it was recognized as containing a summary of the doctrine of the founder of "scientific" Socialism.[7]

Early in 1848 Marx returned to Germany when he heard rumors of revolutions stirring there. At once he began the publication of a radical paper *Neue Rheinische Zeitung*. Again, the government stepped in and charged him with inciting armed resistance. Although Marx was acquitted, he was forced to leave his country. He sought refuge in England where he remained until his death in 1883. During his exile he published *Das Kapital* and organized an international society of workingmen. Its purpose was to propagate his theories.

Although it would be interesting to investigate Marx's theory of dialectical materialism, it is not necessary here. It is sufficient to say that Marx envisioned all the institutions of society, such as the state, Church, and school, as by-products of the economic system of the day. According to Marx, the institution of private property enables some men to seize possession of the bounty of the earth, and hence forces men to work for them. These owners in the course of time have built up a state, Church, and school to enforce and justify, and teach the righteousness of their conduct. Hence, Marx would remove exploitation by removing its cause, property, and its accompanying institutions, the state and the Church. To bring about this removal, a revolution was necessary. And this revolution, he claimed, was provoked by the system itself, which unites the workers and continually aggravates them by more and more exploitation. Thus, the capitalist system will eventually destroy itself.[8] For, through factory exploitation of labor, capitalism will become concentrated, in time, in fewer hands, while the masses of the population will increase and grow more "class-conscious." Eventually, the day will come, when the many will be

[7] Hayes, *op. cit.*, p. 257.

[8] J. J. Cronin, *Economics and Society* (New York: American Book Co., 1939), pp. 187-188.

able to dispossess the few and usher in the proletarian society. Then, the economic means of production and exchange will be owned and operated socially. Then, too, will all the "bourgeois" institutions disappear. In the meantime, it is the business of "scientific Communists" to prepare the proletarians for their inevitable victory, and to encourage them to the "class struggle" which they must wage with capitalists.[9]

The vehicle that first propagated these theories was the International Working Men's Association. Although the organization was started in London in 1862 by English, French and Belgian workers, it was not formally launched until 1864 when it adopted the Marxian teachings. This "First International," as it came to be known, held annual meetings until its dissolution in 1876. Actually, it was an attempt to unite the workers or proletarians of the world.

Neither the death of Marx, nor the death of the First International, however, meant the death of Marxian Socialism. Organizations, Marxian in character, continued to be founded in various nations. The Social Democratic Party in Germany eventually became the model for Marxian societies in other countries. Hence, by the year 1914 practically every civilized nation had a Socialist party whose gospel, at least in theory, was the teaching of Karl Marx.[10] A Second International was founded in 1889 but was disbanded in 1914 when the First World War broke out.

According to Hayes, in estimating the significance of Karl Marx's contributions to the Socialist movement, four facts stand out prominently. He systematized existing social theories. Secondly, he emphasized the political, as well as the economic character of Socialism. Thirdly, he conferred on Socialism a philosophy and a claim to be considered a science. And finally, Karl Marx made his appeal not so much to theorists or philanthropists or altruistic bourgeois, like the Utopian Socialists, as directly to the workingmen themselves.[11]

---

[9] Hayes, *A Political and Cultural History of Modern Europe* (2 vols., New York: Macmillan Co., 1936), II, 377.

[10] Hayes, *A Political and Social History of Modern Europe*, II, 261.

[11] *Ibid.*, p. 260.

Section III. Russia and Communism

Up until the time of the First World War, although there were numerous Socialist or Communist organizations, their activities were limited and sporadic. The two Internationals had been abandoned and what success they did have was of no great importance. Generally speaking, these organizations remained debating societies with no sanction and few effective weapons. Marx and his companion Engels drew up the basic doctrines of Communism, but they supplied few guides to the practical methods of revolution. The man who finally took the Communist theory of Marx and forged it into a Communist organization of action was Nikolai Lenin, the Russian revolutionist. Thoroughly steeped in Marx's teaching, Lenin, more than any other man is the molder of modern-day Communism and the architect of the Party structure.

J. Edgar Hoover, commenting on Lenin's contribution to Communism, says:

> Borrowing from the autocratic character of Marx himself, Lenin made Marxism a highly disciplined, organized, and ruthless creed. How can revolution be achieved? Not by democratic reforms, ballots, or good will but by naked, bloody violence. The sword is the weapon. Everything must be dedicated to this aim: one's time, talents, one's very life. Revolutions do not just happen. They are made.[12]

And the revolution Lenin made took place in Russia. During the winter of 1916-1917 the people of Russia, having long suffered oppression and poverty under the rule of the Tsars, and being now engaged in a World War, broke into open rebellions. There were strikes in the cities, and riots among the peasants. At last, in April of 1917, the weak Imperial rule was overthrown and a provisional government was established. But this proved no stronger than the former, and in November Nikolai Lenin, the fanatical, iron-willed, devout follower of Marx, with the aid of Leon Trotsky and other revolutionaries overthrew the provisional rule. This meant that at last "scientific Socialism" was no longer

---

[12] J. Edgar Hoover, *Masters of Deceit* (New York: Henry Holt & Co., 1958), pp. 28-29.

just a theory; now it had physical control of one of the major governments of the world.

The Lenin Party was small when it gained control that November, but the leader was attuned to the desires of the masses and his program eventually won him support. He proclaimed that his dictatorship was a "dictatorship of the proletariat," including workers, peasants and soldiers; and upon each of these groups he proposed to confer immediate benefits.[13] To attract the industrial workers, he planned the confiscation of private factories to be placed under government control. He enticed the peasants by plans to expropriate lands to be consigned to peasant communities. By signing the Brest-Litovsk Treaty he withdrew from the war and thus won favor with the army. Titles of nobility and all class distinctions were abolished. Measures were taken in January of 1918 to disestablish the Orthodox Church in Russia and to silence all Christian clergymen.[14] The murder of Tsar Nicholas, his wife and children was but the beginning of a long series of purges. The treatment afforded the Church will be seen later.

During the years 1919 and 1920 internal difficulties threatened the Bolshevik regime.[15] Gradually, however, Lenin secured control, and in 1922 the first All Union Congress of Soviets was held. It was at this meeting that the Union of Soviet Nations was formed (U. S. S. R.), comprising four republics. In the same year Germany recognized the Soviet Government, and Great Britain and France followed suit in 1924. The United States gave recognition in 1934.

Section IV. The Third International

In 1919, just two years after the Bolsheviks seized control of Russia, they sent out invitations to attend an international congress

---

[13] Hayes, *A Political and Cultural History of Modern Europe*, II, 908.

[14] *Ibid.*, p. 909.

[15] The term Bolshevik arose quite by accident. At a congress of the illegal Russian Socialist Party, held in London in 1903, Lenin won a majority of votes on an issue. His followers came to be known as "Bolsheviki." *Bolshinstvo* is the Russian word for majority. His opponents became known as "Mensheviki"—the minority. These two factions of the party were continually at odds over aims and policies.—W. Gurian, *Bolshevism* (Notre Dame, Ind.: University of Notre Dame Press, 1952), p. 1.

in Moscow, the new capital of Russia. The purpose of the meeting was to lay plans for the inauguration of a Communist movement on an international scale. Since its purpose was to continue the work originally undertaken by the First International, it referred to itself as the Communist Third International. In time it was also known as the Comintern.

Although Germany at that time had the only Communist party, strictly speaking, outside of Russia, there were numerous left-wing, revolutionary parties in every country. The immediate aim of the Third International was to unite these organizations, strengthen them, and eventually steer them to a world revolution. Communism, as conceived by Marx, was not designed to be bound in by the borders of one country; it was drawn up as a world-wide movement.

The following year, 1920, saw the Second Congress of the Third International. From only a casual reading of the statutes adopted at this meeting, the ultimate goal of the Comintern is apparent. The introduction to the Statutes of the Communist International states:

> In order to overthrow the international bourgeoisie and to create an international Soviet Republic as a transition stage to the complete abolition of the state, the Communist International will use all means at its disposal, including force of arms.[16]

The first statute of the International also states:

> The new International Association of Workers is established for the purpose of organizing common activity of the workers of various countries who are striving towards a single aim: the overthrow of capitalism, the establishment of the dictatorship of the proletariat and of the International Soviet Republic for the complete abolition of classes and the realization of Socialism—this first step to Communist Society.[17]

---

[16] W. Chamberlin, *Blueprint for World Conquest* (Washington, D. C.: Human Events, 1946), p. 35. This valuable book contains reliable translations of early documents of the Third International.

[17] *Ibid.*, p. 36.

In its desire to attract the numerous left-wing groups then existing, the Comintern also drew to itself a number of organizations it considered as undesirable. To correct this, the Second Congress established a policy of making membership in the International difficult to attain. This was accomplished by drawing up twenty-one conditions for admission. They demanded, among other things, centralization of authority in all Communist parties, subordination to the Comintern, periodical purges, and exclusion of members who did not vote for affiliation with the International.[18]

The action of the Second Congress produced a greater unity in the movement, and the International proceeded to renew its revolutionary spirits. During the early 1920's, however, because of the peculiar circumstances of the times, little could be done through revolutions. In fact, with the exception of China, non-Russian Communism was busy protecting itself, rather than taking the offensive.[19] The Communist leaders, aware of the Party's unpopularity, did not launch any major revolutions, but contented themselves with unifying the ranks and preparing for the opportune time.

With the death of Lenin in 1924, tensions among the various factions of the Party inside and outside of Russia came to the surface. Stalin and Trotsky disagreed over internal and external Party problems. Stalin was maintaining his theory of "building Communism in one country." Trotsky leaned more in the direction of promoting world revolution. This is not to say that Stalin was less concerned with world revolution. Rather, it was a question of which should receive greater stress at the time.[20] Stalin won, and Trotsky was ultimately exiled.

The Sixth World Congress of the International, held in Moscow in 1928, greatly unified the movement and revivified its spirit. The Congress drew up an extensive program. The tactics and

---

[18] *Ibid.*, pp. 65-72.

[19] M. Salvadori, *The Rise of Communism* (New York: Henry Holt & Co., 1952), p. 35.

[20] M. Fisher, *Communist Doctrine and the Free World* (Syracuse: Syracuse University Press, 1952), p. 251.

strategy outlined at the meeting laid heavy stress on revolution. Moreover, the Constitution and Rules formulated at that time set down the basis for future Party organization.[21]

By 1935 there were Communist Parties in over fifty countries. About the same time Fascism had gained control of Italy, and Germany had turned to National Socialism. The Communist strategists, realizing that such movements constituted a threat to the advancement of Communism, adopted the policy of "Popular or United Front movement." This program was activated at the Seventh World Congress of the Comintern held in Moscow in 1935. It was at this Congress that Dimitrov gave what has become known as his "Trojan Horse" speech. In a number of places in this speech, Dimitrov expressed his views on the Catholic Church and his plans for attacking the Church.[22]

This new tactic of the United Front was designed to combat Hitler and the growing Fascist movements. The Bolsheviks particularly feared the growing strength of German military power. Hence, they now sought collaboration with Socialist and leftist parties in the various countries to smother the Fascist threats. The Communists no longer spoke of internationalism or class struggle. The great emphasis was now on nationalism and cooperation. It was during this period that the Soviet Union sought membership in the League of Nations (1935), and became a strong supporter of "collective security." Fascism, the Communists shouted, presented a danger to all nations. Hence, all must work together to destroy it.[23]

With the outbreak of the Second World War, and Germany's attack on Russia in June of 1941, the Soviet Union was forced to seek assistance in order to survive. Salvadori says, "The Communists were now willing to collaborate with anyone who was against the Germans and the Nazis."[24]

During the Second World War the Communist Parties in coun-

---

[21] Chamberlin, *op. cit.*, pp. 249-257.

[22] These parts of the speech are re-printed by Lerhinan, J., *A Sociological Commentary on "Divini Redemptoris"* (Washington, D. C.: The Catholic University of America Press, 1946), p. xvii.

[23] Hoover, *op. cit.*, p. 71.

[24] *Op. cit.*, p. 59.

tries under the control of the Axis powers made the most of the situation. Party members cooperated with non-Communist groups and engaged in sabotage and guerrilla warfare against the Axis forces of occupation. This National Front Program, carried on extensively during the War, won the Party a number of allies inasmuch as it appeared as though the Communists were no longer interested in world revolution, but were actually loyal to their respective countries. To further this impression, the Third International was dissolved in May of 1943.

Louis Budenz, former Communist and former editor of the now defunct *Daily Worker,* has this to say about the dissolution of the Comintern:

> The agency which formerly was the channel of directions was the Communist International, known popularly as the Comintern. Founded by Lenin in March, 1919, it was for years the guiding hand that ruled the Red invading armies in all countries. In May, 1943, its dissolution was announced "to advance the fight against Fascism." In actuality, the step was taken by Stalin to soothe the feelings of the United States and to make easier the granting of huge lend-lease aid to Russia. The dissolution, it will be noted, took place in the midst of World War II, when the Moscow dictatorship was hard pressed by the Nazi military machine.[25]

Igor Gouzenko, a cipher clerk attached to the Soviet Embassy in Ottawa, Canada, in a statement made in October, 1945, to the Canadian Royal Commission investigating the Communist spy apparatus in Canada, testified:

> The announcement of the dissolution of the Comintern was probably the greatest farce of the Communists in recent years. Only the name was liquidated, with the object of reassuring public opinion in the democratic countries. Actually the Comintern exists and continues its work.[26]

---

[25] *The Techniques of Communism* (Chicago: Henry Regnery & Co., 1954), pp. 20-21.

[26] This piece of testimony appeared in *Organized Communism in the United States* (a pamphlet prepared and released by the Committee on Un-American Activities, United States House of Representatives, Washington, D. C., United States Government Printing Office, 1953), p. 137.

The favorite Communistic tactic employed in the so-called dissolution of the International will be examined in a later section.[27]

To a large extent the plan for National Fronts was successful. By the end of the Second World War, the Communist Party appeared to many as just another political organization. Party membership increased during the post-war period, and its leaders obtained important positions in the coalition governments being formed in the countries of Europe.

In 1947, the International was revived, but under a new name. It was now the Information Bureau of the Communist Workers' Parties (Cominform). Delegates of the Communist Party in the following countries were present in Poland at the formation of the Bureau: Yugoslavia, Bulgaria, Rumania, Hungary, Poland, France, Czechoslovakia, Italy and the Soviet Union.

Three years after Stalin's death in 1953, at the Twentieth Congress of the Communist Party of the Soviet Union held in 1956, a policy of de-Stalinization was inaugurated. The complete significance of this tactic is not yet fully known by the outside world.[28] One of the points of the program was the dissolution of the Cominform that had been established in 1947 while Stalin was ruling.

The relationship between the International and the Communist Party of the United States should be of interest to Americans. The Constitutions of the American Communist Party adopted in the years 1921, 1925, and 1929 all provided that these Parties were the American section of the Communist International.[29] A new Constitution of the American Communist Party, adopted in 1938, stated that the Party was an *affiliate* of the Communist International.[30] It will be recalled that this was the era of the

---

[27] Cf. *infra*, pp. 21-24.

[28] For the opinions of some of the specialists on the Soviet Union, see *The Great Pretense, A Symposium on Anti-Stalinism and the 20th Congress of the Soviet Communist Party* (a pamphlet prepared and released by the Committee on Un-American Activities, United States House of Representatives, Washington, D. C., 84th Congress, 2nd Session, House Report No. 2189, United States Government Printing Office, 1956).

[29] *Organized Communism in the United States*, pp. 51-80, 89. This work contains the full texts of these Constitutions.

[30] *Ibid.*, p. 99.

United Fronts and the Communist tactic was to tone down the international ambitions of Communism. In 1940, a more drastic revision in the Constitution of the American Party was made. In that year the Congress of the United States passed the Voorhis Act which provided for the registration of all foreign agents who engage in political activity. Inasmuch as the Constitution of the American Communist Party declared that the Party was an affiliate of the International, and since the leaders of the Party were not anxious to register Party members, a special convention of Party leaders was called in New York. At that meeting it was decided to disaffiliate from the International, and the Party's Constitution was so amended.

Earl Browder, the general secretary of the Communist Party at that time, explained that this separation from the Communist International was merely a legalistic step. It was in no way intended to alter the real relationship between the American Communist Party and the Communist International.[31]

ARTICLE 2. THE COMMUNIST PARTY

Section I. Organizational Structure

The Communist Party that is so efficiently and so effectively operating today in all parts of the world was formed and fashioned during that era that began with the Russian revolution in 1917 and ended with the consolidation of Stalin's power in 1927.[32] The structure of this closely-knit, well-regulated organization is outlined in the Constitutions and Rules of the Party.[33]

In order to examine the framework of the organization and appreciate its discipline, it is best to begin at the basic unit of the Party, and then proceed up the chain of command to the top echelon. However, it must be noted that this is the structure of the Communist International Party as it is drawn up in the official Constitutions of the Party which were composed with an eye to public consumption. Moreover, in practice, the accidentals

[31] *Ibid.*, p. 132.

[32] Salvadori, *The Rise of Modern Communism*, p. 43.

[33] Chamberlin, *Blueprint for World Conquest*, pp. 249-258.

of the organization's structure and the manner of operation can vary from country to country, depending on local conditions and the nature of the work to be accomplished. For example, at present the Party in the United States can be compared to an iceberg. A portion of the Party is before the public in order to maintain the fiction that the Communist Party is an open political party. It presents public Party officials and offers candidates for offices in the Government. But the larger section of the Party is submerged and away from public view. On the other hand, during the Second World War, when the Party was displaying its patriotic colors as part of the National Front Program, the Party had a rather large membership and open headquarters.[34] The Party is presently operating in this manner in several European countries.

The basic unit of the Communist Party is the cell or nucleus.[35] These cells are made up of people who work in the same place—factory, store, labor union, etc. In addition to these industrial cells, as they are called, there are street cells which unite Party members living in the same neighborhood. Many countries, because of circumstances, are organized on the basis of residence. Currently, the cell members of the American Communist Party conceal their affiliation with the Party and generally operate in secrecy.[36]

Each of these industrial and street cells is controlled by an executive committee of the chief officers. A group of cells in a given area is under a section committee. The next higher body is the state or district committee, above which is the national committee of the Party. Since the national executive committee will meet only a few times a year, a small body known as a politburo, or presidium, carries on the business during the interval.[37]

---

[34] Budenz, *The Techniques of Communism,* p. 38.

[35] Section 4: "The basic unit of the Communist Party organization is the nucleus. . . ."—Chamberlin, *op. cit.,* p. 250.

[36] For a detailed account of how these cells operate, cf. *The Communist Party of the United States of America* (a pamphlet prepared by the Subcommittee on Internal Security of the Senate Committee on the Judiciary, 84th Congress, 2nd Session, Senate Document No. 117, United States Government Printing Office, 1956).

[37] Budenz: "In studying the Communist apparatus, we must be aware that there is a frequent change of name for the various organs or bodies of the Party, though their respective functions remain the same."—*Op. cit.,* p. 38.

Prior to the alleged dissolution of the Communist International in 1943,[38] each of the Parties operating in the various countries sent delegates to the World Congress held every two years. This World Congress, made up of the delegates from all the national Parties, was the supreme ruling body of the Communist Party.[39] Since the Congress met every two years, during the interim an executive committee, elected by the Congress, performed administrative tasks. However, this committee was granted numerous, rather broad powers. For example it issued instructions to all sections of the International. Moreover, these instructions were obligatory on all.[40] The right to expel from the International entire sections, groups and individual members was also granted to the Committee.[41] When the Executive Committee was in recess, a politburo carried on the administrative duties. Ever since the so-called dissolution of the Communist International in 1943, the functions of the Executive Committee have been carried on, in practice, by the Politburo of the Communist Party of the Soviet Union, in collaboration with a few non-Russian Communists.[42]

Information, directives, and the Party line are frequently transmitted by means of the Communist International Representative whose office is outlined in *Section 22*. These representatives oftentimes bring their instructions from the International Committee to the various national headquarters, as well as to local organizations. In addition to these personal carriers, week by week orders and policies are brought to diverse organs by means of Party magazines and newspapers.

Budenz in his book, *The Techniques of Communism,* devotes

---

[38] Cf. *supra,* p. 14.

[39] Section 8: "The supreme body of the Communist International is the world Congress of representatives of all Parties (Sections) and organizations affiliated to the Communist International."—Chamberlin, *op. cit.,* p. 251.

[40] *Section 13:* "The decisions of the E.C.C.I. are obligatory for all the Sections of the Communist International and must be promptly carried out. The Sections have a right to appeal against the decisions of the E.C.C.I. to the World Congress, but must continue to carry out such decisions pending the decision of the World Congress." *Ibid.,* p. 253.

[41] *Section 15, ibid.,* p. 253.

[42] Salvadori, *op. cit.,* p. 45.

a section to a demonstration of how the Party operated while he was an active member.[43] A brief summary of his description will enable the reader to see how the chain of command functions. Although the International has allegedly been dissolved at various times, witnesses before the Committee on Un-American Activities have disclosed in terms of their experience that the statutes of the Party are still fully operative as the implement of international unity and government.[44]

When Budenz was active in the Party, the national committee met at least four times a year. During these meetings the national leader presented a report containing the changes and new interpretations laid down by Moscow. Thereupon, each member of the national committee expressed his agreement and explained how he planned to execute the orders.

After the national committee meeting, the district or state leaders delivered the report to their subordinates. A discussion was held with them, not concerning the merits of the orders, but how best to put them into action. The report then traveled to section and branch leaders where it was read and further discussed. The same procedure was carried on in the cells.

Briefly, this is the apparatus of the Communist International Party. From Moscow, the nerve center of the Party, flow the directives and strategy to the numerous national committees, thence to the districts, and finally down to the locals. The Constitution and Rules describe this autocratic system by the euphemistic phrase "democratic centralism."[45] According to Communists, Party members have a right to participate in the formulation of policy and electing officers. J. Edgar Hoover exemplifies the process in action. An issue arises. For example, the city is planning to close a playground. What stand should the Party take? All the members are encouraged to express opinions. There may be different points of view. But once the decision has been made, from that moment on, the centralism takes over and the democratic ceases. All members, regardless of their previous

---

[43] *Op. cit.*, pp. 27-28.

[44] *The Communist Party of the United States*, p. 20.

[45] *Section 5, op. cit.*, p. 250.

opinions, are required to support the Party's stand. "No minority can exist."[46]

Obviously, to function properly this whole system demands military-like discipline and devotion to duty. This quality is ensured by continual instructions given to the members on the Party's aims and ambitions, by close surveillance of the members, and by periodic purges to eliminate those who seem to be wavering. The type of punishment the Party inflicts on reactionaries and deviationists depends upon the position and strength the Party enjoys in an individual country.[47]

Section II. Strategy and Tactics of the Party

A. Basic Principles

It is a principle of military science that the strategy and tactics of an army must be constructed in the light of the objective or goal to be secured. For that reason, before examining the strategy and tactics of the Communist movement, it will be helpful to consider the ultimate objective of modern Communism.

The ultimate goal of the Communist Party is clearly set forth in the Program adopted by the Sixth World Congress of the International held in 1928, which Program has never been repealed. The opening sentence of *Article III* of that Program states:

> The ultimate aim of the Communist International is to replace world capitalist economy by a world system of Communism.[48]

In the long section that follows this statement, there is contained a description of the nature of this Communist society. Some of the features are: the State, private property, and all class distinctions will be abolished. Moreover, the Program says this Communist society "will bury forever all mysticism, religion, prejudice and superstition and will give a powerful impetus to the development of all-conquering scientific knowledge."[49]

---

[46] *Masters of Deceit,* p. 144.

[47] *Ibid.,* pp. 173-188 for methods of punishment.

[48] Chamberlin, *Blueprint for World Conquest,* p. 179.

[49] *Ibid.,* p. 181.

The ultimate aim, then, of the Communist Party is to overthrow the present world of nations and replace it with the Communist classless, Godless society. However, this upheaval of society, says the Program, is not to come over night. Rather, the world is to pass through a period of transition, involving a series of revolutions in one country after another, establishing proletarian dictatorships. In time, these will give way to the Communist society.

Therefore, the primary purpose of a Communist party in any given country is to work towards the realization of the nation's revolution. And these individual efforts of the various parties over the world are coordinated by the World Congress of the International, or whatever body is taking its place. Just how the parties and the International are to accomplish this turnover of society is a question of strategy and tactics.

The Program of the World Congress of 1928 presents an elaborate plan to be followed by the Party in fomenting, organizing, and successfully executing the revolutions. Since a detailed analysis of the plans would require more space than the topic demands in a work of this nature, only an outline can be presented here. However, special emphasis will be placed on the basic characteristic of the plan.

If one word can be selected to describe the fundamental characteristic of the Communist plans for world revolution, it is the word *adaptability*. The designers of the Program realized that as the Party moves across the world, organizing revolutions, it will of necessity be operating in countries widely divergent—economically, socially, and culturally. For that reason, the Program presents three main plans of attack, depending on the type of country. As the Program states:

> The variety of conditions and way by which the proletariat will achieve its dictatorship in the various countries may be divided schematically into three main types: countries of highly developed capitalism (United States of America, Germany, Great Britain, etc.) . . . countries with a medium development of capitalism (Spain, Portugal, Poland, Hungary, the Balkan countries, etc.) . . . . Colonial and semi-colonial countries

(China, India, etc.) and dependent countries (Argentina, Brazil, etc.). . . .[50]

For each of these three main types of countries, the Program sets down a general pattern to follow and general aims to achieve. It also devotes a special section to the more backward, primitive countries. As to the specific means of achieving the immediate aims set forth in the various categories, the Program again stresses the need for adaptability.

> . . . each Communist Party must take into account the concrete internal and external situation, the correlation of class forces, the degree of stability and strength of the bourgeoisie, the degree of preparedness of the proletariat. . . . The Party determines its slogans and methods of struggle in accordance with these circumstances. . . .[51]

A few examples will be presented to demonstrate the various methods employed by the Party. In the poorer countries, especially where there is present some degree of despotism and oppression, the Party sets out to incite strife and discontent by fanning local quarrels, hatreds, and dissensions. Strikes flare out and eventually open rebellion. In the midst of the confusion and disorder, the masses all too quickly will accept any cohesive force that promises to relieve the situation and fulfill their desires. Communism presents itself as such a force, and to make itself more acceptable, it cleverly designs its propaganda to create the impression that the Party is entirely altruistic, interested only in restoring peace, justice and equality for the downtrodden masses.[52]

In countries where comparative peace and prosperity exist and where public opinion is not favorable to Communism, the Party oftentimes operates underground, or behind the scenes, as it is now

---

[50] *Ibid.*, pp. 209-210.

[51] *Ibid.*, p. 238.

[52] Cf. Pius XI, encycl. *Divini Redemptoris:* "For those who promote this cause employing the specious appearance of truth, claim that they truly desire only to bring about a better condition of the working people. . . ."—*AAS*, XXIX (1937), 72.

doing in the United States.[53] In the industrial countries, the Party seeks to gain control of trade unions and other organizations of the workers.[54] In the colonial and semi-colonial countries, for example, it agitates for independence, for agrarian reforms, and especially the Party must "combat the reactionary and medieval influence of the clergy, of the missionaries and other similar elements."[55] The Party also makes use of groups known as "Front Organizations." However a special section will be devoted to them, and their purpose and function will be considered at that point.[56]

Contemporaneously with its efforts to infiltrate into the organizations of the workers, or agitate unrest, the Party is always operating its highly developed propaganda machine. By numerous means the Party pumps its heavily veiled, hardly discernible propaganda into the various sections of society, gradually breaking down the resistance to Communism. Pius XI describes the Party's use of propaganda in this way:

> And this propaganda, flowing from one source, is adapted craftily to the special circumstances of peoples; it makes use of huge sums of money, countless societies, international conventions, close-knit and well-organized groups; and likewise, bit by bit, through newspapers, pamphlets, motion pictures, the stage and the radio, and finally through schools and universities it infiltrates into all, even the better classes of society, and without their realizing it, poisons their minds and hearts.[57]

---

[53] Speaking before the subcommittee of the House Committee on Appropriations on Dec. 9, 1953, J. Edgar Hoover, Director of the Federal Bureau of Investigation, described the current organization of the Communist Party in America: "No longer are Communist Party membership cards issued; maintenance of membership records are forbidden. . . . Most of the local headquarters have been discontinued and party records have been destroyed. . . . Conventions and large meetings are held to the absolute minimum. The use of the telephone and telegraph is avoided." Quoted in *The Communist Party of the United States,* p. 19.

[54] Chamberlin, *op. cit.,* p. 235.

[55] *Ibid.,* p. 238.

[56] Cf. *infra,* pp. 34-40.

[57] Encycl. *Divini Redemptoris—AAS,* XXIX (1937), 72; translation from Lerhinan, *A Sociological Commentary on "Divini Redemptoris,"* p. 28.

In its open relations with the world in general and nations in particular, this principle of adaptability is employed with much success. Lenin, the master strategist of the revolution, stressed the need for flexibility of tactics when he wrote:

> The strictest loyalty to the ideas of Communism must be combined with the ability to make all the necessary practical compromises, to "tack," to make agreements, zig-zag, retreats, and so on.[58]

This principle can be found underlying all of the Communist Party's policies. For example from 1935 to 1939 Russia was strongly anti-fascist, and strove to erect "popular fronts" against Nazi aggression. In 1939 the Soviets about-faced and signed a non-aggression pact with Hitler. Until 1936 the Chinese Communists opposed Chiang Kai-shek; in 1937 they established a united front with him. During the Second World War the Party temporarily dropped its more extreme doctrines and championed nationalism and cooperation. In short, if the Party foresees that by signing this treaty, or by making that concession, or righteously upholding some policy today, and roundly condemning it tomorrow, it will better its position, then that action can and must be taken. Since the Communist has no moral code, nor even the semblance of the natural virtues of justice, honesty, and integrity, he suffers no pains of conscience.

This tactic, among other things, is calculated to create the impression that the Party has at last seen the folly of its ways and now desires to live in peace and concord with the rest of the world. It is made to appear as though the Party has changed its fundamental principles and aims, when in fact, it has merely made a tactical shift.

B. Strategy and Tactics Employed Against the Church

A summary of the techniques employed by the Communist Party in its war against the Church will further exemplify the above mentioned principles.

---

[58] *Left Wing Communism* (New York: International Publishers, 1934), p. 138.

It is fundamental that since Communism is based on materialistic philosophy it must be opposed to the supernatural. The Program adopted in 1928 leaves no doubt as to its position on religion:

> One of the most important tasks of the cultural revolution affecting the wide masses, is the task of systematically and unswervingly combating religion—the opium of the people.[59]

That Communism is opposed to religion can also be readily realized by observing the movement in action. Religious persecutions in Russia varied in intensity from 1917 until the beginning of the Second World War. Between 1917 and 1922 an intense anti-religious campaign was waged. Church property was confiscated; schools were closed, and clergymen were exiled or murdered.[60] A second wave struck in 1929, and a third in 1937.

Since 1938, however, a number of factors have caused the Soviets to alter their attack against religion. For one thing, the leaders have discovered that religion can not be eliminated with one bold strike. And too, with the rise of Fascism, the Soviet Union was in desperate need of assistance from other countries. Realizing that these persecutions were having adverse effects on the outside word, the Party toned down its attack against religion. Again, it was not a change in basic principles. The Party simply decided to liquidate religion in a more subtle manner, and at the same time win the friends it sought.

Today, in many of the countries directly under the Communist rule, the Party's attack on the Church proceeds according to the principle of adaptability. That is, before the Party takes any steps against the Church, it first takes into account a number of circumstances—the intensity of Christian life, the number of Catholics in the country, and the amount of resistance the people

---

[59] Chamberlin, *op. cit.*, pp. 207-208.

[60] *Communism in Action* (A Documented Study and Analysis of Communism in Operation in the Soviet Union, prepared at the instance and under the direction of Representative Everett M. Dirksen of Illinois, by the Legislative Reference Service of The Library of Congress, 79th Congress, 2nd Session, House Document No. 754, United States Government Printing Office, 1946), p. 127.

offer to Communist propaganda. If the country offers too much resistance to the propaganda, and severe measures would only result in disturbing the economic order by work stoppages, etc., the Party moves more cautiously.

In those countries where a direct, all-out persecution would prove to militate against the best interests of the Party, nationally or internationally, the Communists would nevertheless attempt by other means to render the Church ineffectual. A number of methods are employed to accomplish this purpose. However, one of the more successful is to launch a quiet attack against the unity and organization of the Church. This method is described in a recently published book, written by a priest who lived under the Communist rule in Central Europe. According to this author the Communists attempt to destroy the unity of the Church in the following manner:

> 1) Above all by breaking the unity with Rome, by preventing contact of the hierarchy and the faithful with this center of the Catholic Church. At the same time by skilful propaganda must be undermined the respect and affection of the clergy and faithful toward the Holy Father,
> 2) by breaking up the unity of the bishops among themselves,
> 3) by breaking up the unity between bishops and priests,
> 4) by breaking up the unity of the priests among themselves,
> 5) by breaking up the unity of the clergy and the faithful.[61]

The author proceeds to demonstrate the various tactics which the Party uses to bring about these various dissensions. One of the methods employed actually has a threefold result. The Party, realizing the influence the clergy has over the faithful, attempts to entice the clergy to exercise their influence in behalf of the State. Oftentimes the projects for which they seek the clergy's

[61] A. Michel, *Dividing the Church* (London, Sword of the Spirit, 1956), Original title, *Problemes Religieux dans un Pays sous Regime Communiste* (Paris, Editions Fleurus, 1955), p. 9.

assistance are social projects in themselves good.[62] But by busying the clergy with purely secular tasks, it takes away, or at least diminishes their spiritual activity.

The second result is that it creates favorable propaganda in the outside world if the Party is pictured as dealing kindly with the Church.

The third result comes in this way. In order to get the clergy to cooperate with the State, the officials offer to rebuild churches, equip seminaries, or they promise to grant some material benefits to the clergy.[63] What the party asks in return seems very slight inasmuch as the projects are praiseworthy. But once the pattern of compromise is established, the demands gradually increase. If a sufficiently large number of compromising priests can be found, they are formed into clubs such as the Union of National Priests, or the Catholic Priests of Peace. The presence of these clubs naturally creates a division between the loyal clergy and the so-called "patriotic priests." The latter also cause untold scandal among the faithful.

Another technique used to separate the Church is the office of Ecclesiastical Affairs. On the surface this bureau is designed to coordinate relations between Church and State. In practice it reduces the Church to a department of the State. For it often happens that "stubborn" officials of the Church are removed from office and replaced by "patriotic priests" who are named as vicars general. Inevitably confusion results from the fact that such priests are not canonically appointed to their positions. Moreover these "patriotic priests" will hardly have the best interest of the Church at heart.

When the State removes those of the clergy who will not cooperate, they are normally tried and convicted for anti-social, and anti-national crimes. But the Party avoids giving the impression that such clergy are being punished for their religious

---

[62] Pius XI spoke of a similar tactic when he wrote: "Thus it has happened in some places, that, not at all rejecting their own beliefs, they have united with Catholics for some cultural or charitable purposes."—Encycl. *Divini Redemptoris*, *AAS*, XXIX (1937), 102. Cf. also A. Galter, *The Red Book of the Persecuted Church* (Westminster, Md., The Newman Press, 1957).

[63] Michel, *op. cit.*, p. 5.

activity. If the faithful do get the impression that the penal action is directed against religion, the Party line shifts to the theme that it is not against religion, only its abuses.

Finally, at times the State finds it necessary to seek the assistance of the Catholics. For example, in Hungary in 1953 and 1955 the country was faced with an economic crisis. To gain the support of the Catholic population, the Communists eased the pressures previously enforced on the faithful. Another tactic it uses to solicit assistance, a variation of the one just mentioned, is to launch severe measures against the Church, followed by a period of calm and apparent truce. This too creates the impression that the regime has abandoned its plan to destroy the Church, and the people become more amenable to accept the policies the Party is attempting to foster.

These and other tactics, too numerous to mention here, are daily being used to liquidate the Church in a quiet manner. In addition to these clever maneuverings, the Party is constantly feeding its propaganda to the people, giving special attention to the youth. At the same time the Catholic press is silenced, schools are closed, or carefully watched, and priests who preach against the existing government are soon reported to the authorities. In considering the question of those who in some way affiliate with the Communist Party, pressures such as these must be recalled.

Section III. Membership in the Party

Both the Communist theorists and the official documents of the Communist Party indicate that formal membership in the Party is not open to all. Various reasons necessitate this procedure. First of all, the very nature and role of the Party, namely, that it is to be the vanguard, the inspiration and guiding and driving force of the revolution, calls for a selective group.[64] Secondly, the high

[64] J. Stalin: "Every army at war must have an experienced General Staff if it is to avoid certain defeat. All the more reason therefore why the proletariat must have such a General Staff if it is to prevent itself from being routed by its mortal enemies. But where is the General Staff? Only the revolutionary party of the proletariat can serve as the General Staff."—*Leninism* (2 vols., New York: International Publishers, no date of publication), I, 89.

degree of discipline and organization required calls for a small, compact, easily manageable group.[65] Finally, the theorists of the movement looked upon the members of the vanguard—the Party—as a special class of people. Stalin expressed this conviction in his address at the bier of Lenin.

> We communists are people of a special mold. We are made of special stuff. We are those who form the army of the great proletarian strategist, the army of Comrade Lenin.[66]

For the most part this feeling of being esoteric was provoked by the impression that the vast horizons and complex principles of the Communist movement were too profound for the ordinary proletariat to grasp.[67]

The Constitution adopted by the Sixth World Congress of the International reflects this need for selectivity of members by establishing certain conditions for entry into the Party.

> Membership of the Communist Party and of the Communist International is open to all those who accept the program and rules of the given Communist Party and of the Communist International, who join one of the basic units of a Party, actively work in it, abide by all the decisions of the Party and of the Communist International, and regularly pay Party dues.[68]

Several examples will demonstrate the means the Party has used at various times to maintain this "proper type of personnel." According to a report from the United States Department of Defense, applicants for membership in the Party of the Soviet

---

[65] N. Lenin: "The only serious organizational principle the active workers of our movement can accept is: strict secrecy, strict selection of members, and the training of professional revolutionists."—*What Is To Be Done* (New York, International Publishers, 1929), p. 131.

[66] J. Stalin, *History of the Communist Party of the Soviet Union (Bolshevik)* (New York, International Publishers, 1939), p. 268.

[67] G. Almond, *The Appeals of Communism* (Princeton, N. J., Princeton University Press, 1954), p. 9.

[68] Chamberlin, *Blueprint for World Conquest*, p. 249.

Union are examined in the following manner.[69] The applicant must be sponsored by at least three persons who have been Party members in good standing for three years or more, and who have known the applicant for at least one year. Moreover, the political beliefs as well as the private life and personal character of the candidate are thoroughly examined. If he is accepted, a period of probation follows. This lasts a year, during which time he is kept under close surveillance. If he passes this examination, full membership is granted to him. To prevent sponsorship from being taken lightly, sharp reprimands—if not more—are given to the sponsors if the applicant fails.

The Constitution of the Communist Party of the United States, adopted in 1945, also establishes conditions for membership. The article on members reads in part:

> Section 1. Any resident of the United States, 18 years of age or over, regardless of race, color, national origin, sex, or religious belief, who subscribes to the principles and purposes of the Communist Party, shall be eligible for membership.
>
> Section 2. Any person eligible for membership according to Section 1, who accepts the aims, principles and program of the Party as determined by its constitution and conventions, who holds membership in and attends club meetings, who is active on behalf of the Party, who reads the Party literature and pays dues regularly, shall be considered a member.
>
> Section 3. An applicant for membership shall be endorsed by at least one member of the Communist Party. Such application is subject to discussion and decision by the Club to which it is presented.[70]

The theory, therefore, of the Party is that it should be extremely cautious in admitting potential members into its ranks. To insure this, the Party frequently demands periods of probation as well as periods of indoctrination.

---

[69] *Know Your Communist Enemy* (a series of pamphlets published by the Office of Armed Forces Information and Education, Department of Defense, Washington, D. C., n. 4, *In the Iron Grip of the Kremlin,* 1955, United States Government Printing Office), pp. 13-14.

[70] *Organized Communism in the United States,* p. 123.

The following chart prepared by the Senate Committee on Foreign Relations, May 1954, gives some indication of the size of the Party in countries outside the Soviet bloc.[71]

Country	Members
Italy	1,700,000
France	450,000
W. Germany and Berlin	195,000
Japan	80,000
Austria	60,000
Brazil	60,000
Argentina	*30,000
Chile	*50,000
India	40,000
United Kingdom	*34,801
Netherlands	33,000
Belgium	*30,000
Cuba	*30,000
Finland	30,000
Sweden	30,000
United States	25,000
Greece	20,000
Venezuela	*27,000
Algeria	15,000
Indonesia	15,000

*Claimed by Communist Party.

It will be noticed that certain countries, for example, France and Italy, have an unusually large number of members in comparison to other countries. This is partially explained by their many complex problems, involving social, economic and political factors. However, the tactics employed by the Party in those areas also provides some explanation.

It was ssen in the previous section[72] that the Party is not adverse to shifting its attack when circumstances and the over-all good of the Party warrant it. This is what the Party has done in a number of countries as regards its policy on membership. For many reasons, some known only to the strategists of the movement, the Party has currently, in various parts of the world,

---

[71] Reprinted in *Know Your Communist Enemy* (n. 4 *International Communism, Its Teachings, Aims and Methods,* 1954), p. 13.

[72] Cf. *supra*, pp. 21-24.

opened wide its doors. It conducts extensive campaigns for membership; only slight qualifications are demanded, if any at all, and all sorts and types of persons are readily admitted.

An interesting study has been made by Professor Gabriel Almond, and published under the auspices of the Center of International Studies of Princeton University. This work gives a detailed presentation of the numerous cleverly devised propaganda techniques the Party has recourse to during these periods of the open Party.[73]

The Party, realizing that it could never attract the masses by simply and boldly advertising that it intends to establish a classless, Godless society, and that all are welcomed to join in the overthrow of the present order, has set about to entice members by a more gentle approach. It is well aware that a direct appeal clearly stating its objectives and means would shock and horrify the average person. And too, it realizes that the worker is generally not concerned with long range plans. His vision is usually limited to his own little world and the problems he daily faces.

Consequently, the Party's propaganda emphasizes local needs, and points up the problems, contentions and inequalities existing among the peoples it is attempting to attract. Temporarily, it makes no mention of the true motives of the Party, nor does it stress the connection between these minor objectives and the final goal it is seeking. In addition to underlining the local deficiencies, it presents itself as the paragon of virtue, and identifies itself with the goals of the particular people it is attempting to win.[74] All the conclusions of the Princeton study are based on data acquired from former Communists. Those in England and the United States claimed they joined the Party because it represented a means of achieving trade union objectives and a general social improvement. Those in France and Italy stated that the goals presented by the Party coincided with the "social humanitarian aspirations which were deeply rooted in those countries before the advent of Communism."[75]

---

[73] Almond, *op. cit.*, chap. 3.

[74] *Ibid.*, p. 79.

[75] *Ibid.*, p. 104 .

One former Communist testified that the reason the appeal of Communism is so strong is that 99 per cent of its propaganda has nothing to do with Communism. "Communist propaganda is 99 per cent aggressive, critical, and there is so much to criticize in the *status quo* that the propaganda is bound to be effective. . . . They can win all kinds of people with real grievances."[76]

In conjunction with this propaganda the Party also offers, when possible, material inducements to entice potential members. The Party pays expenses and tuitions for the more active Communist students in universities, or they offer lucrative positions in the Party.[77] In countries where the Party has control of unions, it does not hesitate to use this power as a means of forcing laborers to enter the Party by making Party membership a requisite for work.

In short the Party has one form of propaganda geared for the intellectuals, another for the workers, another for the youth, and so on. The whole program is rather well summed up by the study made by Professor Almond under the auspices of the Center of International Studies of Princeton University. The study says:

> . . . At the point of entrance into the movement, the Party is all things to all men. It tempts the workman with an image of the alert and militant trade unionist, concerned with the pragmatic and immediate needs of the working class. It confronts the peasant with the ideal of the militant defender of the rights of the small farmer and farm laborer. It offers the intellectual the tempting model of the artist or writer employing his talents effectively in the cause of social justice. It offers the native colonial the image of the militant patriot driving the imperialist before him, wiping out the indignities of centuries of exploitation and humiliation. And before all potential party recruits and supporters, it holds up the generalized image of the militant and effective reformer locked in battle with injustice.[78]

---

[76] *Ibid.*, p. 128.
[77] *Ibid.*, p. 237.
[78] *Ibid.*, p. 5.

Twenty years ago, Pius XI warned the world of this technique when he wrote in his encyclical on atheistic Communism:

> In the beginning Communism showed itself as it really was, a thing more vicious than the most vicious. But immediately realizing that it was everywhere alienating people from itself, it changed its method of warfare and endeavored to deceive the masses through falsehoods of various kinds which purposely were hidden in teachings in themselves good and attractive.
>
> Thus, for example, the Communist leaders, recognizing that there is a universal desire for peace, pretend to be the most zealous of all men in support of the common effort to maintain peace among all nations.[79]

The result of this program of mass enrollment now being conducted in various parts of the world has been to some extent deceiving. It is true that numerically the Party has swelled. However, this does not mean that all of these taken into the Party are ideal members. In actual practice the Party is still guided and controlled by a hard core of dedicated, indoctrinated Party militants—the elite, esoteric group described by the original Communist theorists. Outside of this inner circle is the mass of rank and file members, and evidence seems to indicate that there is a chasm between the two.[80] Nevertheless, the Party attempts to indoctrinate the outer group by means of national, or regional schools, or local study groups. Those who seem to be more promising are gradually assimilated into the higher echelons, or inner circle.[81]

Section IV. Communist Fronts and Party Sympathizers

To complete this brief sketch of the Communist Party in action it is necessary to consider two other means the Party frequently employs to advance its causes and widen its sphere of influence. These means are the Communist Fronts and Party sympathizers.

---

[79] Encycl. *Divini Redemptoris—AAS,* XXIX (1937), 95; translation from Lerhinan, *A Sociological Commentary on "Divini Redemptoris,"* p. 112.

[80] Almond, *op. cit.*, p. 169.

[81] *Ibid.*, p. 112.

J. Edgar Hoover defines a Communist Front as "an organization which the Communists openly or secretly control."[82] The best way to appreciate the nature and the purpose of these organizations known as "Fronts" and to understand the reason for their success is to try to visualize the problems the Party faces when it launches its attack against a country.

Generally speaking the Party will be relatively small in membership, as was seen in the previous Section. Moreover, the doctrines and ultimate goal of the Communist Party are for the most part contrary to the very nature of man, and hence most people, if they realize the full import of the Communist teachings, will bitterly oppose them. Therefore, the Party must a) attempt to gain assistance from people outside the Party, and b) conceal the true objective of Communism. Over the course of years the Party has found that one of the best means of achieving both these ends is the Front organization. Consequently, one of the first steps that Party takes when it moves into a country is to establish one of these groups.

Benjamin Gitlow, former Communist Party candidate for Vice President of the United States, former member of the Party politbureau, and former member of the Executive Committee of the Communist International, testified before the United States Congress' Special Committee on Un-American Activities that these front organizations are established in the following manner.

> First, a number of sympathizers who are close to the Party and whom the Party knows can be depended upon to carry out Party orders, are gotten together and formed into a nucleus which issues a call for the organization of a particular front organization which the Party wants to establish. And generally after that is done a program is drawn up by the Party, which this provisional committee adopts. Then, on the basis of this provisional program, all kinds of individuals are canvassed to become sponsors of the organization, which is to be launched in the very near future. A provisional secretary is appointed before the organization is launched and in every instance in our day the secretary who was appointed was a member of the Communist Party. . . . And as presi-

[82] *Masters of Deceit*, p. 228.

> dent of the organization we would put up some prominent public figure who was willing to accept the presidency of the organization, generally making sure that, if that public figure was one who would not go along with the Communists, he was of such a type that he would be too busy to pay attention to the affairs of the organization.[83]

Eventually, the Party will have a network of these organizations operating in the country. In the United States each of these fronts is affiliated with a parent international front from which the national and local groups receive instructions, literature, etc., in order to coordinate the various organizations and disseminate the ever-changing Party policy.[84] Some of the more prominent national and international organizations that have been established are:

American Youth for Democracy
Congress of American Women
American Committee for Protection of Foreign Born
World Federation of Democratic Youth
International Union of Students
World Federation of Democratic Women
World Peace Congress
World Federation of Scientific Workers
International Organization of Democratic Journalists
International Association of Democratic Lawyers.[85]

The names of the organizations mentioned above indicate several characteristics of the fronts. First, the names in no way show that the group is affiliated with the Communist Party. Secondly, these fronts invariably select titles that give the impression the organization is dedicated to some great humanitarian cause, e.g., American Youth for Democracy, American Committee for Protection of Foreign Born, World Peace Congress.[86] This is the provisional

---

[83] This part of Gitlow's testimony is reprinted in the Senate Subcommittee Study: *The Communist Party of the United States of America,* p. 93.

[84] *Loc. cit.*

[85] *Ibid.,* pp. 91, 93.

[86] Cf. also Pius XI, encycl. *Divini Redemptoris:* "Under various names which do not even suggest Communism, they establish organizations and periodicals with the sole purpose of carrying their ideas into quarters otherwise inaccessible."—*AAS,* XXIX (1937), 95.

program which Gitlow stated the nucleus of the front presents to potential sponsors.[87]

At times these fronts will assume names that are very similar to well-known and respectable organizations. The Senate Subcommittee report gives the example of the front organization which operated under the name, The Methodist Federation for Social Action. Actually this organization had no official connection with the Methodist Church.[88] A number of these Communist fronts also make it a practice to change their names from time to time.[89]

A third characteristic indicated by the names of the fronts listed above is that these organizations quite often are established to appeal to special groups, e.g., lawyers, women, youth, journalists, etc.[90]

The real, but cleverly concealed objectives of these fronts can be manifold. For example, certain Communist fronts in America pour Communist theories and misinformation into the streams of public opinion. According to the Senate Subcommittee Study this was the purpose of the Allied Labor News Service, the Federated Press, and the Labor Research Association.[91]

The Party has also used these fronts to present its candidates for public office. By having a candidate for office sponsored by some organization which gives no indication of being related to the Communist Party, the danger of alienating non-Communist voters is lessened.[92]

The Party can also, by means of these fronts, quickly mobilize what appears to be a body of public opinion outside the Party. This technique is commonly used to promote some piece of legislation favorable to Communists. Since one front will support another, the Party can pyramid the membership, thus giving the impression that large numbers of people support the proposed program.[93] Moreover, these fronts carry an array of prominent

---

[87] Cf. *supra*, p. 35.

[88] *The Communist Party of the United States*, p. 96.

[89] *Ibid.*, p. 93.

[90] *Loc. cit.*

[91] *Ibid.*, p. 91.

[92] *Loc. cit.*

[93] *Ibid.*, p. 92.

sponsors, as Gitlow testified.[94] Such names lend an appearance of respectability to the fronts, and can be extremely helpful in swinging public opinion.

A further benefit the Party derives from these fronts is that they provide excellent recruiting grounds for new Party members.[95] Almond, in his survey of former Communists, states that of the 221 former Party members interviewed 54 per cent had joined a front organization before entering the Party proper.[96]

In addition to the fronts which the Party establishes, it also attempts to infiltrate into already existing non-Communist organizations. Members of the Party will join these organizations, for example, trade unions, and then set about to seize control of key positions. Once they have acquired these positions, by means of skillful parliamentary procedure, techniques of leadership and propaganda, such members of the Party are able to manipulate the organization to sponsor or favor various drives being conducted by the Party. This is particularly easy when the non-Communist members are indifferent as to the welfare of their organization.[97] Budenz sums up the influence and importance of these Party members who infiltrate into non-Communist organizations.

> One member of the vanguard could thereby become as a thousand men, moving hundreds of thousands of people unwittingly into action according to the Kremlin's wishes.[98]

The people attracted to these front organizations are termed by the Senate Subcommittee Study, "fellow travelers." The term "fellow-traveler" is derived from the Russian word *poputchiki* meaning "travelers on the same road." It became popular at the time of the Bolshevik revolution in Russia. At that time the Communists were judiciously placing a few non-Party sympathizers

---

[94] Cf. *supra*, p. 36.

[95] *Ibid.*, p. 92.

[96] Almond, *The Appeals of Communism*, p. 224.

[97] *Know Your Communist Enemy* (n. 4. *International Communism: Its Teachings, Aims and Methods*), p. 14.

[98] *Techniques of Communism*, p. 153.

in positions of prestige in order to create the impression that the Communist regime controlling the government had popular support.[99]

With the passage of time the term has come to signify all types of Party sympathizers. The Senate Subcommittee Study, however, restricts the term to those who join these Communist Fronts. And there are two general types. The "conscious fellow-traveler," according to the Senate Subcommittee, is one who joins or supports one or more of these fronts, fully aware that the organization is operated and directed by the Communist Party. For the most part, such persons have a definite sympathy for the Communist Party or the Soviet Union or both.[100]

The second type is a person the Senate Subcommittee describes as an "unwitting fellow-traveler." Such a person joins the front under the mistaken impression that the organization is actually dedicated to some praiseworthy program, and has no knowledge of the organization's connection with the Communist Party.[101]

In addition to establishing these fronts, the Party, when it organizes its attack against a particular country, will also make special appeals to the various types of Communist sympathizers outside the Party and outside the fronts. The Senate Subcommittee divides these sympathizers into two groups.[102]

Nonparty Communist: A nonparty Communist is one who is sympathetic to the Communist movement, but for some reason he finds it inadvisable or inexpedient to join the Party. For example, persons of great wealth or prominence will not be able to attend the meetings of the Party and fulfill the other duties required by formal membership, but they submit themselves to the Party's wishes and desires.[103]

Communist Party Supporter: This person is distinguished from the above by the fact that the Communist Party Supporter is in no way under the direction of the Party. But the Communist

---

[99] Sidney Hook, "The Fellow Traveler: A Study in Psychology—" The New York Times Magazine, April 17, 1949, p. 9.

[100] *Art. cit.*, p. 32.

[101] *Loc. cit.*

[102] *Ibid.*, p. 32.

[103] *Loc. cit.*

Supporter voluntarily and knowingly supports the Communists in one or more ways such as voting for Communist candidates, signing of Communist election petitions, donating money for the Party press, supporting organizations openly sponsored by the Communist Party, doing organizational and political favors for the Party, or writing for the Communist press.[104]

By the assistance of these front organizations and with the aid given by Communist sympathizers, the Party is able to exercise influence far out of proportion to its actual membership.

---

[104] *Loc. cit.*

CHAPTER II

Papal Statements on Communism

INTRODUCTION

A review of the papal statements on Communism at once reveals that the popes, the Vicars of Christ on earth, have from the earliest days of the Communist movement seen its basic fallacies and inherent threats to civilization. Moreover, these statements provide ample proof that the popes have consistently taken a positive stand against Communism, even at times when Communist strategy and tactics had succeeded in deceiving numerous nations, and creating an atmosphere in which criticism of Communism was looked on with disfavor. A review of these statements also results in the disheartening conclusion that had the world given more attention to the continuous warnings of the popes, much of the present-day sorrow and suffering could have been avoided.

ARTICLE 1. THE NINETEENTH CENTURY

Section I. Pope Pius IX

The first specific reference to atheistic Communism in a papal statement appears in the nineteenth century in the encyclical of Pius IX, *Qui Pluribus* (1846).[1] This was issued five months after he ascended the Chair of Peter. The message opens with an expression of the Pope's desire to discharge with fidelity the duties of a successor of Peter. He speaks of his anxiety to protect the Church, Her rights and privileges. He describes the deplorable conditions of human society and strongly condemns Rationalism and the right of private interpretation of Scripture. He then presents a list of monstrous errors, among which he includes Communism and describes it as a doctrine "totally contrary to even

[1] Pius IX, encycl. *Qui Pluribus*, 9 Nov. 1846—*Fontes*, II, n. 504, 807-817.

the natural law itself, and which, once accepted, would utterly destroy personal rights, private property, and rights of ownership of all, and even human society itself."[2]

The fact that this encyclical appeared two years before the *Communist Manifesto* demonstrates that Pius IX was well aware of the dangerous doctrines being propagated by the small but vociferous group of Socialists. It was seen in the first chapter[3] that the early part of the nineteenth century saw the rise of the Socialist movement in order to remedy the multitude of injustices created by the spirit of economic individualism: low wages, intolerable working conditions, and the great unequal distribution of wealth. In 1841 Feuerbach had published his *Essence of Christianity* in which he formulated his philosophy of materialistic monism. The previous year saw the release of Proudhon's work, *What Is Property?* an attempt to translate social problems into terms of Hegelianism. Proudhon and Bakunin, representing the more extreme group of Socialists, were calling for a destruction of private property and all authoritarian government. However, all these disparate efforts were basically atheistic and materialistic.

Three years later, Pius IX, in his allocution *Quibus Quantisque,*[4] again attacked Communism. The previous year had been a crucial one for all Europe. Revolutions had spread from one country to the next, so that "within a few months half the monarchs of Europe had either been deposed or forced to concede constitutions."[5] Pius IX had been forced to flee Rome and take up residence in Gaeta. A number of Socialist groups, particularly those headed by Blanc and Proudhon, took an active part in some of these rebellions. Blanc, in fact, was given a voice in the new fusion government established in France. Marx at this time was living in Paris, but hearing that the revolutionary wave was moving over Germany, returned to Cologne in 1848 and set up his radical *Neue Rheinische Zeitung.*[6] Although these Socialist and Com-

---

[2] *Ibid.,* p. 811.

[3] Cf. *supra,* pp. 5-8.

[4] Pius IX, allocut. *Quibus Quantisque,* 20 April, 1849—*Fontes,* II, n. 507, 823-837.

[5] Hayes, *A Political and Social History of Modern Europe,* I, 123.

[6] Cf. *supra,* p. 7.

munist groups (at this time the terms were interchangeable) did precipitate some of the revolutionary movements,[7] it cannot be said that they were the actual cause of all the numerous uprisings or political changes taking place in that tumultuous year, 1848. Rather, they were but an element in some instances of the growing democratic movement that was gradually rising to replace the traditional monarchical governments.

The particular allocution under consideration, *Quibus Quantisque,* was issued by Pius IX while at Gaeta. Rome was under the control of Mazzini, assisted by Garibaldi and a number of other revolutionaries. At a special meeting of the illegal Constituent Assembly of the revolutionary government[8] held in Rome on February 9, 1849, it was voted to end the temporal power of the Pope and establish a "pure democracy."[9]

Two months after this meeting of the Assembly, Pius IX, in this allocution, *Quibus Quantisque,* explicitly condemned those who were pretending that abrogation of the temporal power of the Pope would serve the good of the Church. This was the reason given by the Assembly for its action. He laments the fact that the Holy City is swarming with apostates, heretics, *Communists* and Socialists who, animated by a supreme hatred for the Catholic Truth, are attempting to spread their pestiferous errors and corrupt the minds of men.[10]

In December of the same year, 1849, Pius IX sent an allocution to the archbishops and bishops of Italy in which he summarized the attempts being made to undermine religion in their country.[11] One section is devoted to Communism and Socialism, and it is highly important because it displays the Pope's keen awareness of the tactics being used by the Communists to achieve their objectives.[12] He warns the Italian hierarchy that the Communists

[7] Hayes, *op. cit.*, p. 255.

[8] E. Hales, *Pio Nono* (New York: P. J. Kenedy, 1954), p. 128. This author explains why this so-called Constituent Assembly of the People of Rome was actually illegal.

[9] *Ibid.*, p. 98.

[10] *Allocut. cit.*, p. 831.

[11] Pius IX, allocut. *Nostis Nobiscum,* 5 Dec. 1849—*Fontes,* II, n. 508, 837-849.

[12] *Ibid.*, p. 843.

and Socialists are attempting, by a misuse of the terms of liberty and equality, to spread their destructive lies among the people. Moreover, the Pope warns that although the leaders of the Communists and Socialists employ diverse methods and approaches, their purpose is the same. They excite continuous agitation among the workers and the people of the lower classes, who, deceived by the Communist lies and promises of better conditions, gradually are encouraged to commit more grave crimes. Eventually, the Communists are able to use the masses to attack authority, to plunder, first the property of the Church, and then that of others. In time, the masses are driven to violate all divine and human rights, to destroy divine worship, and ultimately to overthrow the whole of society.[13] Obviously, reports had reached the Pope of the seizure of convents and religious property to be used by the army. He was no doubt informed of the blasphemous processions that were taking place in the city, and of the several priests who were murdered by the revolutionaries.[14]

Pius then admonishes the hierarchy to instruct the faithful lest they be deceived by these foes of the Church and civilization. And later he solemnly warns that those who conspire with the Communists and Socialists should know and seriously consider the punishments God will inflict on them.[15]

The next important papal condemnation of Communism is to be found in another encyclical of Pius IX, *Quanta Cura,* December 8, 1864.[16] In this encyclical Pius IX adds a new reason for condemning Communism, namely, its attack upon the family.

> Not content with abolishing religion in public society, they desire further to banish it from families and private life. Teaching and professing these most fatal errors of

[13] ". . . ut postmodum illorum opera uti possint ad superioris cuiusque Auctoritatis regimen oppugnandum, ad expilandas, diripiendas vel invadendas Ecclesiae primum, ac deinde aliorum quorumcumque proprietates, ad omnia tandem violanda divina humanaque iura, in divini cultus destructionem atque in subversionem totius ordinis civilium Societatum."—*Loc. cit.*

[14] Hales is of the opinion that the plunder was not as great and as intense as was reported to the Pope.—*Op. cit.,* pp. 125-126.

[15] *Allocut. cit.,* p. 845.

[16] Pius IX, encycl. *Quanta cura,* 8 Dec. 1864—*Fontes,* II, n. 542, 993-999.

> Socialism and Communism they declare that "domestic society, or the family, derives all its reason of existence solely from the civil law. . . ."[17]

The *Communist Manifesto* expresses this attitude towards the family in these words:

> Abolition of the family! Even the most radical flare up at this infamous proposal of the Communists. On what foundation is the present family, the bourgeois family, based? On capital, on private gain. In its completely developed form this family exists only among the bourgeoisie. But this state of things finds its complement in the practical absence of the family among the proletarians, and in public prostitution. The bourgeois family will vanish as a matter of course when its complement vanishes, and both will vanish with the vanishing of capital. Do you charge us with wanting to stop the exploitation of children by their parents? To this crime we plead guilty.
>
> But you will say, we destroy the most hallowed of relations, when we replace home education by social. The bourgeoise clap-trap about the family and education, about the hallowed co-relation of parent and child, becomes all the more disgusting, the more, by the action of Modern Industry, all family ties among the proletarians are torn asunder, and their children transformed into simple articles of commerce and instruments of labor.[18]

It should be recalled that by this time, 1864, the *Manifesto* had been in circulation for almost fifteen years, and was being adopted by a number of the left-wing parties of Europe.

Toward the end of this encyclical, *Quanta Cura,* Pius IX leaves no doubt as to the status of the various errors mentioned in his message, among which is Communism.

> Therefore do We, by our Apostolic authority, reprobate, denounce and condemn generally and particularly all the evil opinions and doctrines specially mentioned in this letter, and We wish that they be held as reprobated, de-

---

[17] *Ibid.,* p. 996.

[18] Marx, *Communist Manifesto,* pp. 28-29.

> nounced and condemned by all the children of the Catholic Church.[19]

Pius IX appended his famous *Syllabus of Errors* to this encyclical. The *Syllabus* contains a compilation of the ten major errors afflicting society. Communism is listed in the fourth class along with Socialism and secret societies.[20] Cardinal Antonelli, in a letter accompanying the encyclical and the Syllabus, explains why the Syllabus is being sent to the bishops:

> But as may happen that all the pontifical acts do not reach each one of the ordinaries, the same Sovereign Pontiff has willed that a Syllabus of the same errors be compiled, to be sent to all the bishops of the Catholic world, in order that these same bishops may have before their eyes all the errors and pernicious doctrines which we have reprobated and condemned.[21]

In short, the Pope was doing as much as possible to make certain the bishops were aware of the Church's attitude towards these various current trends.

Section II. Pope Leo XIII

After the year 1870 the Marxian doctrines secured a large following because his approach to the current social problems seemed "timely." It was advertised as "scientific," and it was frankly materialistic, enshrining concepts of struggle and evolution. This naturally appealed to the "realistic" nineteenth century.

On April 21, 1878, Pope Leo XIII, shortly after his election, issued his first encyclical, *Inscrutabili,*[22] in which he outlined the various evils penetrating modern society. The following December his famous encyclical on Socialism, Communism and Nihilism ap-

---

[19] *Encycl. cit.,* p. 997.

[20] "IV—Socialismi, Communismus, Societates clandestinae, Societates biblicae, Societates clerico-liberales."—Pius IX, *Syllabus errorum—Fontes,* II, n. 543, 1002.

[21] Letter from Card. Antonelli—*Acta Sanctae Sedis* (41 vols., Romae, 1865-1908), III (1865), 167-168 (hereafter cited as *ASS*).

[22] Leo XIII, encycl. *Inscrutabili,* 21 April, 1878—*Fontes,* III, n. 573.

peared, *Quod Apostolici.* The reason for this encyclical, says Pope Leo, is that the evils which he condemned in his first encyclical, *Inscrutabili,* have made such rapid advancement that he is compelled to address his flock anew.[23] Although he did not mention Communism by name in his first encyclical, he does so in *Quod Apostolici.* After a brief introduction in which he explains the reason for writing this encyclical, Leo says:

> You understand as a matter of course, Venerable Brothers, that We are alluding to that sect of men who, under the motley and all but barbarous terms and titles of Socialists, Communists, and Nihilists, are spread abroad throughout the world and, bound intimately together in baneful alliance, no longer look for support in secret meetings held in darksome places, but standing forth openly and boldly in the light of day, strive to carry out the purpose long resolved upon, of uprooting the foundations of civilized society at large.[24]

Leo makes four charges against these groups. First, they openly and boldly strive to overthrow civilized society. Secondly, they do away with obedience to authority and preach perfect equality of all men in regard rights and duties. Thirdly, they destroy the sacredness of marriage, and finally, they attack the right of private property.[25] Of all the papal statements on Communism, this encyclical contains some of the strongest language.

A later encyclical of Leo XIII, condemning Freemasonry touches on the relationship between this movement and Communism.[26] The first reference to Communism appears in paragraph n. 6 where he says:

> We have several times already, as occasion served, attacked certain chief points of teaching which showed in a special manner the perverse influence of Masonic opinions. Thus in Our encyclical letter *Quod apostolici*

[23] *Fontes,* III, n. 576.

[24] *Loc. cit.;* translation from *The Great Encyclical Letters of Pope Leo XIII* (New York: Benziger Bros., 1903), p. 22.

[25] *Loc. cit.*

[26] Leo XIII, encycl. *Humanum genus,* 20 April, 1884—*Fontes,* III, n. 591.

> *muneris,* We endeavored to refute the monstrous doctrines of the Socialists and Communists. . . .[27]

The second reference to the connection between Masonry and Communism is found in paragraph n. 18.

> Now, from the disturbing errors which We have described the greatest dangers to States are to be feared. For, the fear of God and reverence for divine laws being taken away, the authority of rulers despised, sedition permitted and approved, and the popular passions urged on to lawlessness, with no restraint save that of punishment, a change and overthrow of all things will necessarily follow. Yea, this change and overthrow is deliberately planned and put forward by many associations of *Communists* and *Socialists;* and to their undertakings the sect of Freemasons is not hostile, but gravely favors their designs, and holds in common with them their chief opinions.[28]

ARTICLE 2. THE TWENTIETH CENTURY

Section I. Pope Pius XI

The pontificate of Pius XI was especially concerned with Communism. When Achille Cardinal Ratti became Pius XI in 1922, the Bolshevik government under Lenin was well entrenched in Russia, and Pius soon saw the major powers of the world accepting the Union of Soviet Republics as a respectable nation. Moreover, he also observed Communism spreading out from Russia, year by year increasing its numbers, intensity and influence. Finally, during his fifteen years as Pope he was forced to stand by and watch thousands of his flock persecuted and murdered by the Communists in Russia, Spain and Mexico.

In April 1922, the first year of his pontificate, the great powers of Europe met with the Bolshevik government at the International Conference held in Genoa. Although the Holy See was not invited to attend, Pius XI sent papal diplomats to the conference to urge the Allies not to accept the Bolshevik government into the

---

[27] *Ibid.,* p. 223.

[28] *Ibid.,* p. 230; translation from *The Great Encyclical Letters of Pope Leo XIII,* p. 99.

union unless it guaranteed freedom of religion in Russia and returned the confiscated Church property. Although his suggestions went unheeded, he was able to make an agreement with Russia to allow the Holy See to send assistance to the millions starving to death in the great famine of Russia.[29] This Papal Relief Mission remained in Russia until 1924 when the Soviet government declared it no longer needed foreign assistance. It is estimated that the Holy See expended close to $1,500,000 in this act of charity to the Russian people.[30]

After this Papal Relief Mission returned in 1924, Pius XI made his first pronouncement on Communism. It appears in an allocution dealing with a number of varied subjects.[31] Concerning the situation in Russia, he speaks with deep feeling for the people suffering from the famine there, and tells of the efforts made by the Papal Relief Mission to assist these people. He then adds:

> Let it not appear to anyone that, because of Our charity (of which We have spoken) exercised among the Russian people, We have favored in any way the form of government which is so far from having Our approval that on the contrary, We who have directed Our thoughts and energetic efforts for so long a time in relieving such great evils among that people, think it pertains to the office of common paternity given to Us by God, to warn all and especially rulers of peoples and to exhort them vigorously in the Lord that all who love the public prosperity and peace and who are supporters of the sanctity of the family and of human dignity, strive with united energies to remove from themselves and their peoples the most grave and certainly threatening dangers and evils arising from what are called Communism and Socialism (having due care and regard for improving the condition of workingmen and in general of all men of the lower classes).[32]

[29] W. Teeling, *Pope Pius XI and World Affairs* (New York: F. Stokes Co., 1937), p. 107.

[30] E. Walsh, *Why the Pope Asked Prayers for Russia on March 19, 1930* ([no place of publication indicated] The Catholics Near East Welfare Assoc., 1930), p. 22.

[31] Pius XI, allocut., 18 Dec., 1924—*AAS,* XVI (1924), 489-497.

[32] *Ibid.,* pp. 494-495; translation from Lerhinan, *A Sociological Commentary on "Divini Redemptoris,"* p. 16.

Lerhinan, in his commentary on the encyclical *Divini Redemptoris,* points out that there are several important ideas contained in this sentence.[33] First, there is contained here a condemnation of the form of government existing in Russia. According to Lerhinan, this seems to be the first time the Holy See ever condemned a form of government. Secondly, this statement of Pius XI gives proof that the Church was concerned not only with the economic aspect of Communism but especially with its attacks on the family and the dignity of the individual. Finally, it demonstrates that the Pope clearly distinguished between the Russian people and their rulers or form of government.[34]

In 1930 Pius XI directed that the Leonine prayers recited after the Sacrifice of the Mass be offered for the Church in Russia, and he instructed the bishops to remind the faithful of this intention from time to time.[35]

The next explicit mention of Communism in a papal document appears in the monumental encyclical on the restoration of the Christian social order, *Quadragesimo Anno.* This was issued by Pius XI on May 15, 1931.[36] Speaking of Socialism, he says:

> One section of Socialism has undergone approximately the same change through which, as We have described, the capitalistic economic regime has passed; it has degenerated into Communism. Communism teaches and pursues a twofold aim: Merciless class warfare and complete abolition of private ownership, and this it does not in secret and by hidden methods, but openly, publicly, and by every means, even the most violent. To obtain these ends, Communists shrink from nothing and fear nothing; and when they have attained power it is portentous beyond belief how cruel and inhuman they show themselves to be. Evidence for this is the ghastly destruction and ruin with which they have laid waste immense tracts of Eastern Europe and Asia, while their antagonism and

---

[33] Lerhinan, *op. cit.,* p. 17.

[34] *Loc. cit.*

[35] Pius XI, allocut. 30 June, 1930, *AAS,* XXII (1930), 301.

[36] Pius XI, encycl. *Quadragesimo anno,* 15 May, 1931—AAS, XXIII (1931), 177-228.

> open hostility to holy Church and to God himself are, alas! but too well known and proved by their deeds.[37]

Ever since 1917 the Church in Mexico has suffered periodic persecutions. The Constitution, forced upon the people in 1917 by the radical commander-in-chief of the army, Obregon, contained ecclesiastical restrictions.[38] In 1926 a number of laws were enacted which denied practically all rights of religion. In 1929 the government consented to a truce with the Church and made some concessions.[39] However, in 1931 a new persecution broke out. The papal delegate, a native of Mexico, was expelled as a "pernicious foreigner."[40] On this occasion Pius XI issued his encyclical *Acerba Animi.*[41] In the section describing the various means the purveyors of irreligion are using to spread their teachings, e.g., the press, and education, the Pope recalls the necessity of giving the "utmost attention to the education and formation of the young—especially among the poorer classes, since they are most exposed to atheist, masonic, and *Communist* propaganda."[42]

At the Seventh World Congress of the Communist International held in 1935, the program of the Popular Front was adopted.[43] An indication that Pius XI was well aware of this change in tactics by the Communist Party is found in his address at the opening of the International Press Exposition in 1936. He warns that the Communists are making use of underground propaganda especially in Russia, Mexico, Spain, Uruguay, and Brazil. Moreover, the movement has become dangerous, he notes, because lately it has become less violent in its actions in order to penetrate into regions hitherto inaccessible.[44]

Pius delivered this admonition on May 12, 1936. On the 31st

---

[37] *Ibid.*, 213; translation from J. Husslein, *Social Wellsprings* (2 vols., Milwaukee: Bruce Publishing Co., 1943), II, 218.

[38] Hayes, *A Political and Cultural History of Modern Europe,* II, 1084.

[39] *Loc. cit.*

[40] *Loc. cit.*

[41] Pius XI, encycl. *Acerba Animi,* 29 Sept. 1932—*AAS,* XXIV (1932), 321-332.

[42] *Ibid.,* p. 326. (Italics inserted.)

[43] Cf. *supra,* pp. 13-16.

[44] Pius XI, sermo, 12 May, 1936—*AAS,* XXIX (1937), 142-143.

of that same month, while addressing the leaders of Catholic Action, he returned to the subject of the new tactics being used by the Communists. He warned that false interpretations were being placed on the remarks he had made on May 12th. Pius cited the case of a certain paper, claiming the honor of being Catholic, that had so construed his words as to give the impression that it was possible for the Catholic Church to collaborate with Communism. Once again he stressed that this was not possible.[45]

Despite these warnings, a group of "revolutionary Christians," as they called themselves, continued to publish a magazine called *Terre Novelle*. It was eventually put on the Index in July of that year, 1936.[46] Although the Holy Office does not explain exactly why the magazine was condemned, the second paragraph of the decree gives some indication. It states that the Holy Office takes this occasion to warn the faithful about books, papers and periodicals which cunningly defend collaboration between Catholics and Communists, especially under the pretext of encouraging friendly cooperation in charitable works.[47]

Another indication of Pius' concern over the results the Com-

---

[45] This address did not appear in the *Acta*, but it was printed in full in *Periodica de Re Morali, Canonica, Liturgica.* The pertinent section reads: ". . . sciunt omnes quod aliquot abhinc dies exposuimus de periculis quae toti societati civili—hoc etiam expresse elocuti sumus: toti societati civili—incumbunt ex communismo, ubique grassante, ubique serpente, ubique insidiante. Non defuit diarium impressum, diarium quod catholici nominis honorem sibi attribuit, diarium quod sententiam nostram ita retulit, quasi non judicaverimus, vel obliti simus, vel non tam gravia censuerimus communismi pericula in religionem; prout existere possit aut possibilis videatur aliqua compositio inter veritatem sanctae catholicae religionis et hanc omnium humanorum divinorumque jurium negationem, quae est in communismo."—*Periodica de Re Morali, Canonica, Liturgica* (*Periodica de Religiosis et Missionariis*, Brugis, 1905-1919; *Periodica de Re Canonica et Morali, utilia praesertim Religiosis et Missionariis*, Brugis, 1920-1927; *Periodica de Re Morali, Canonica, Liturgica*, Brugis, 1927-1936; Romae, 1937-   ), XXV (1936), 119-120 (hereafter cited as *Periodica*).

[46] S.S.C.S. Off., Decretum, 23 July 1936—*AAS*, XXVIII (1936), 294.

[47] "Hac occasione capta, ispi Emi Patres monent fideles, ut caveant ab omnibus libris, publicationibus diariis, periodicis et aliis editis scriptis insidiose propugnantibus (praesertim sub praetextu amicalis cooperationis in charitatis operibus fovendis) collaborationem catholicorum cum communismi asseclis."—*Loc. cit.*

munists were achieving through their new strategy is the fact that the following September, 1936, in an address to a group of Spanish refugees he again made mention of these deceitful tactics and warned against cooperation with this movement.

> It is not superfluous, on the other hand, but rather it is opportune and even necessary and for Us a duty, to warn against all the insidiousness with which the heralds of the forces of subversion are seeking to find some common ground for possible approach and collaboration on the part of Catholics, and this on the basis of a distinction between ideology and application, between ideas and actions, between the economic and moral order. This insidiousness is dangerous in the extreme and its purpose is purely and simply to deceive and disarm Europe and the world in favor of an unchanging program of hate, subversion and destruction by which they are threatened.[48]

Finally, in 1937 Pius XI devoted an entire encyclical to Communism.[49] The salutation appearing at the beginning of the encyclical states that the Pope is addressing his words to the Patriarchs, Primates, Archbishops, Bishops and other Ordinaries.[50] The reason for writing this encyclical is mentioned in § 6.

> Nevertheless, although We have published repeated paternal exhortations of this kind which you, Venerable Brethren, through so many pastoral letters, even jointly issued, have made known and carefully explained to the Faithful, still the crisis, brought about by the cunning of revolutionaries, daily becomes more and more serious. Wherefore, We have considered it a duty to raise Our voice again; and We do it by means of this solemn document as is the custom of this Apostolic See, the teacher of truth. . . .[51]

By this time it was evident to the Pope that more and more people were succumbing to the new policy of the Communists.

---

[48] Pius XI, sermo, *La vostra presenza,* 14 Sept. 1936—*AAS,* XXVIII (1936), 376-377; translation is from Lerhinan, *op. cit.,* p. 22.

[49] Pius XI, encycl. *Divini Redemptoris,* 31 March, 1937—*AAS,* XXIX (1937), 65-106.

[50] *Ibid.,* p. 65.

[51] *Ibid.,* p. 68; translation is from Lerhinan, *op. cit.,* p. 6.

The shift in Party tactics had all too quickly succeeded in creating the impression that the Communists were no longer interested in world conquest, but were now anxious to live and work side by side with others.[52] The primary purpose of the encyclical, then, is to clear away this smoke-screen of propaganda the Communists had spread across the world, and permit the world to see and realize the true purposes and objectives of the Communist movement. That is why Pius, throughout the course of the encyclical, repeatedly assails the insidious strategy of the Communists which is designed to ensnare the unsuspecting. For example, the Pope says in § 8:

> The Communism of today, more emphatically than similar movements in the past, conceals in itself a false messianic idea. A pseudo-ideal of justice, of equality, and fraternity in labor impregnates all its doctrine and activity with a deceptive mysticism, which communicates a zealous and contagious enthusiasm to the multitudes entrapped by delusive promises.[53]

In a later section he speaks of the teachings of Communism which "though often propounded in a deceitful and enticing form, actually are based upon those principles which Karl Marx propagated concerning materialism. . . ."[54] In answer to the question why such a doctrine spread so rapidly and so widely, Pius replies, "Altogether too few have been able to realize what the Communists want and what they are actually aiming at; while many instead yield to its deception concealed by glowing promises."[55]

---

[52] Cf. *supra*, pp. 12-13.

[53] *Ibid.*, p. 69; translation from Husslein, *op. cit.*, p. 343.

[54] "Iamvero, quae *communistae* hodie impertiunt praecepta, captiosa interdum allicientique specie proposita, iis reapse innituntur principiis quae de *materialismo*, ut aiunt, dialectico atque historico C. Marxius prodidit. . . ." —*Loc. cit.*

[55] "At undenam evenit, ut eadem doctrina, quam et optima studia iam diu exsuperarunt, et cotidianae res omnino refutant, tam celeriter per universum terrarum orbem propagari queat? Id intelligere fas erit, si animo reputaverimus nimium sane paucos, quid velint et quo reapse tendant *communistae*, inspicere potuisse funditus; cum, contra, bene multi callidis eorum sollicitationibus, quas miris pollicitationibus confirmant, facile concedant."—*Ibid.*, p. 72.

In two later sections Pius treats at length this shift in Communist strategy. By way of example:

> In the beginning Communism showed itself for what it was in all its perversity; but very soon it realized that it was thus alienating people. It has therefore changed its tactics, and strives to entice the multitudes by trickery of various forms, hiding its real designs behind ideas that in themselves are good and attractive.[56]

In a final effort to sweep away any doubt or confusion that might remain concerning the Church's position regarding cooperation or collaboration with this diabolical movement, Pius states in clear unmistakable language:

> Venerable Brethren, take the greatest precaution that the Faithful avoid these snares. Since Communism is intrinsically evil whoever wants to save Christianity and civilization from destruction must refrain from aiding it in the prosecution of any project whatever.[57]

Section II. Pope Pius XII

The late Pius XII, following the course of his predecessors, similarly pointed out the abyss to which Communism will lead modern civilization. However, from the review of the papal statements presented in the previous sections, it should be evident that the popes have from the earliest days of the Communist movement clearly seen and consistently warned the world of this disastrous philosophy. The present section on the pontificate of Pius XII will be devoted to a presentation of the condemnations of Communism

---

[56] "*Communismus* initio, ut re erat vera, scelestiorem, quam quod scelestissimum, se praebuit; at cum subinde sensisset ab se populos passim abalienari, ratione belli gerendi mutata, multitudines per eiusmodi varii generis fallacias captare nisus est, quae, quid ipsae intendant, doctrinis occultant in se rectis atque illecebrosis."—*Ibid.*, p. 95.

[57] "Agitedum, Venerabiles Fratres, date impensissime operam, ut fideles ab insidiis caveant. *Communismus* cum intrinsecus sit pravus, eidem nulla in re est adiutrix opera ab eo commodanda, cui sit propositum ab excidio Christianum civilemque cultum vindicare."—*Ibid.*, p. 96.

made by the various Roman Congregations, as well as a brief account of the background of these decrees.

Upon completion of the Second World War in 1945, Soviet Russia and the International Communist Party enjoyed a most advantageous position. From the agreements which had been entered into with the Allies, Soviet Russia not only retained all the territories annexed during the years of Nazi-Soviet cooperation—part of Finland, Estonia, Latvia, Lithuania, eastern Poland and part of Rumania—but the Soviet Union was allowed to include in its orbit of influence the remaining sections of Finland, Poland and Rumania. In addition her control extended to Czecho-Slovakia, Hungary, Yugoslavia, Bulgaria and Albania. Part of East Prussia and Carpo-Ruthenia were incorporated and the Soviet Government occupied large sections of Germany and Austria. This meant that close to sixty million Catholics came under Communist control.[58]

Generally speaking, the Soviet Union at the close of the war enjoyed no small amount of admiration for the battle it had put up against the invading Naxi troops and the successful campaign it had launched in Eastern Germany. Moreover, it had reinstated the Patriarch of Moscow for the Orthodox Church and was giving the impression that it was slowly beginning to grant religious freedom.

The Communist Party at the close of the war was looked upon with less suspicion and at times was openly courted. It will be recalled that the International had been abandoned at the height of the war in 1943[59] as part of the National Front Program. And too, during the war the Communist Parties in the various countries of Axis Europe took active parts in the resistance movements. In short, at the close of the war the Communist Party was appearing as just another political party, interested in helping to solve the problems of post war Europe. Evidence of this can be found in the first elections held in France in 1945. The Party

[58] Hallecki and Murray, *Pius XII: Eugenio Pacelli, Pope of Peace* (New York: Farrar, Strauss and Young, Inc., 1951), p. 243; *cf.* also Salvadori, *The Rise of Modern Communism*, p. 63.

[59] Cf. *supra*, pp. 13-14.

before the war could count on one out of seven votes. In the 1945 election it secured more than one-fourth of the votes.[60]

In Italy Communist ministers were given seats in the coalition governments from 1944 to 1947. At the general elections in 1945, the Party received a little less than one-fifth of the votes, and under the leadership of Togliatti, Party membership went over the million mark.[61] In fact the Communist campaign in Italy had been so successful that the political elections to be held in 1948 would decide whether Italy was to become another Communist controlled state or remain a democracy. The history of these elections provides another chapter in the story of the Church's unrelenting efforts to overcome the threat of Communism.

Prior to these elections of 1948, Pius XII energetically set about to warn the faithful of the gravity of the situation and to instruct them on their obligations to defeat Communism. As Camille Cianfarra, the Vatican correspondent for *The New York Times,* wrote, "He (Pius XII) galvanized the whole clergy—from Cardinals to parish priests—into action."[62] In his pastoral exhortation to the Roman clergy and Lenten preachers in March of that year[63] he emphasized the duty of the clergy to inform the faithful of the extraordinary importance of the forthcoming elections and the moral obligations to vote.

> Everyone must vote according to the dictates of his conscience. Now it is evident that the voice of one's conscience urges every Catholic to give his vote to those candidates or electoral lists that offer really sufficient guarantees for the safeguarding of the rights of God and his soul, for the true welfare of individuals, or families and of society in keeping with God's law and Christian morals.[64]

Four days previously the Sacred Consistorial Congregation

---

[60] Salvadori, *op. cit.,* p. 81.

[61] *Loc. cit.*

[62] *The Vatican and the Kremlin* (New York: E. P. Dutton & Co., 1950), p. 235.

[63] Pius XII, hort., 10 March 1948—*AAS,* XXXX (1948), 116-120.

[64] *Ibid.,* p. 119.

asked the bishops of Italy to remind the faithful of their obligation to vote.

> The Sacred Consistorial Congregation, in consideration of the dangers to which religion and public welfare are exposed, the gravity of which calls for the united collaboration of all honest people, warns all those who have a right to vote, of whatever condition, sex or age, without exception, and who are in conscience strictly and gravely obliged, to use that right.[65]

The Vice-Secretary of the Communist Party in Italy immediately denounced this action as a trick to get votes. He also took occasion to remind the Italian people that the Communists had a thousand times over professed their respect for all religions.[66]

The Communist Party was also actively campaigning and did not hesitate to employ numerous stratagems, many of which met with considerable success among the less educated people. In the province of Reggio Calabria, the Communists began their meetings by making the Sign of the Cross. When the bells of the nearby church announced that Mass was to begin, the Communist suspended the meeting and attended Mass with the crowd. After Mass the rally would continue.[67]

The efforts of Pius XII and the Catholic hierarchy of Italy were successful. The Communist and left-wing Socialists received less than one-third of the votes cast. However, although the returns showed that the Christian Democratic Party achieved an absolute majority in the Chamber of Deputies, the returns also revealed that the coalition formed by the Communists, left-wing Socialists and other extreme groups managed to mass more than 8,000,000 votes. And a large portion of these, it must be remembered, represent Catholic votes. Hence, it meant that many of the faithful, plagued by economic troubles, were impressed by the Communist propaganda promising speedy elimination of their

---

[65] This decree does not appear in the *Acta* but was printed in *The Tablet* (London, 1840—) Vol. 191 (1948), n. 5624, p. 154.

[66] *Loc. cit.*

[67] Cianfarra, *op. cit.*, p. 239. This author provides several other examples of the tactics used by the Communists in this election.

social problems. In addition, because of the ignorance of the people and the clever appeals made by the Communists, many saw no difficulty in being a Catholic and at the same time a member of the Communist Party.

The situation prevailed not only in Italy, but in a number of other European countries. Moreover, the pressures and techniques being applied by the Soviets behind the Iron Curtain were making cooperation with Communism more and more a problem for the Holy See.

In order to check this dangerous attitude rapidly spreading among the faithful, on July 1, 1949, the Supreme Sacred Congregation of the Holy Office issued a decree in which the faithful were reminded of the sanction the Church imposes on those who profess, defend, or propagate the materialistic, anti-Christian doctrine of Communism. This *Decree of 1949*, as it will henceforth be called in this work, was issued in the form of four questions and answers.

> The following questions were asked of the Holy Office:
>
> 1) Whether it is licit to join the Communist Party or to favor it.
>
> 2) Whether it is licit to publish, propagate, or read books, periodicals, daily papers, or sheets which promote the doctrine or action of Communists, or to write in them.
>
> 3) Whether the faithful who knowingly and freely do the acts mentioned in 1 and 2 can be admitted to the sacraments.
>
> 4) Whether the faithful who profess the materialistic and anti-Christian doctrine of Communists, and especially those who defend or propagate it, incur *ipso facto* as apostates from the Catholic faith the excommunication specially reserved to the Holy See.
>
> The Eminent and Most Reverend Fathers who are in charge of the safeguarding of faith and morals, after hearing the opinions of the Reverend Consultors, in the plenary session of Tuesday (instead of Wednesday) the 28th of June, 1949, decided to reply:
>
> 1) In the *negative*: for Communism is materialistic and anti-Christian; and the leaders of the Communists, even though they sometimes verbally profess that they are not attacking religion, in fact nevertheless by doctrine

and action show themselves to be enemies of God and of the true religion and the Church of Christ.

2) In the *negative:* for they are forbidden *ipso iure* (cf. c. 1399 of the Code of Canon Law).

3) In the *negative,* according to the ordinary principles governing the refusal of the sacraments to those who are not properly disposed.

4) *In the affirmative.*

On the following Thursday, the 30th of the same month and year, His Holiness by divine Providence Pope Pius XII, in the customary audience granted to the Most Excellent and Most Reverend Assessor of the Holy Office, approved the resolution referred to him by the Eminent Fathers and ordered that it be promulgated in the official Commentary, *Acta Apostolicae Sedis.*

Given at Rome, the 1st of July, 1949.[68]

A month later, August 11, 1949, the Holy Office issued a declaration concerning the celebration of marriages with Communists.

A Declaration of the Holy Office regarding the celebration of the marriage of Communists:

It has been asked whether the exclusion of Communists from the use of the Sacraments, prescribed by the Decree of the Holy Office of 1 July, 1949, implies also exclusion from the celebration of marriage; and if not, whether the marriages of Communists are governed by the provisions of canons 1060-1061.

On this matter the Holy Office declares: In view of the peculiar nature of the Sacrament of matrimony, whose ministers are the contracting parties themselves and in which the priest acts as a witness *ex officio,* the priest can assist at the marriages of Communists according to canons 1065 and 1066.

But in the marriages of the persons referred to in n. 4 of the aforesaid Decree, the provisions of canons 1061, 1102, and 1109, § 3, are to be observed.

Given from the Holy Office, 11 August, 1949.[69]

---

[68] S.S.C.S. Off., decr., 1 July, 1949—*AAS,* XXXXI (1949), 334; Bouscaren, *The Canon Law Digest* (3 vols., and supplement through 1956, Milwaukee, Bruce & Co., 1934—1943—1953—1954—1955), III, 658-659 (hereafter cited *Digest*).

[69] S.S.C.S. Off., declar., 11 Aug., 1949—*AAS,* XXXXI (1949), 427; *Digest,* III, 407-408.

The following year, 1950, the same Congregation issued a decree regarding the education of children by Communist associations.

> A *Monitum* of the Holy Office:
>
> Some associations have been set up, under the pressure and leadership, as everyone knows, of the Communist party, which have for their purpose to imbue boys and girls with principles and training which are materialistic and contrary to Christian morality and faith.
>
> The faithful are therefore warned that such associations, whatever be the name under which they disguise themselves, are subject to the sanctions mentioned in the Decree of the Holy Office issued on 1st of July, 1949.
>
> 1. Hence parents or those who stand in their place, who contrary to canon 1372, § 2 and the above mentioned Decree of the Holy Office, turn their children over to the aforesaid associations to be trained, cannot be admitted to the reception of the sacraments.
>
> 2. Those who teach boys and girls what is contrary to faith and to Christian morals incur an excommunication specially reserved to the Holy See.
>
> 3. The boys and girls themselves, as long as they have part in these associations, cannot be admitted to the Sacraments.
>
> Given at Rome, from the Holy Office, 28 July, 1950.[70]

The "associations" referred to in this *Monitum* are organizations founded by the Communist Party for youths in countries on both sides of the Iron Curtain, for example, the Association of Italian Pioneers, and the Czecho-Slovakian Youth Organization. These associations, under the direction of the Party, not only propagate Communist errors and calumnies against the Church, they also encourage the children to engage in all forms of immorality.[71]

In addition to these above mentioned decrees, the various Roman Congregations have also issued a number of decrees pertaining to particular situations existing behind the Iron Curtain. Since the Soviet Program to destroy the Church varies only slightly from country to country, it will be sufficient here to consider some of

---

[70] S.S.C.S. Off., mon., 28 July, 1950—*AAS*, XXXXII (1950), 553; *Digest*, III, 660-661.

[71] M. Fábregas, "Annotationes," *Periodica*, XXXIX (1950), 310-314.

the more frequent crimes committed against the Church in those countries, and the action taken by the Holy See. Some familiarity with the problems facing the clergy and laity living under Communist rule will be helpful in the discussions on cooperation that will follow in subsequent chapters.

As was seen in the first chapter,[72] the Communists in time came to the realization that all-out persecutions of the Church frequently proved to be more of a hindrance to the overall strategy of the Party. For that reason the Communist tactics concentrated on the organizing of "national" Catholic churches. By this method, the Party attempts to separate the Church in a given country from the Supreme authority of the Pope. If this can be accomplished the so-called national church falls under the Soviet control and hence the process of final liquidation can be more easily brought about.

To accomplish this nationalization of the Church in the countries behind the Iron Curtain, the Communists launch two simultaneous attacks. One has as its objective the overthrow of the hierarchical organization of the Church. The second attack is directed against the Oriental Churches united to Rome. The main purpose of this offensive is to sever the bond between the Holy See and the Uniate Churches and place these same Churches under the Russian Orthodox Church. This is the same as placing them under Soviet control since the Russian Orthodox Church is today nothing more than a tool of the Red Government. The attack on the Church in Rumania exemplifies this program.

At the close of the Second World War there were an estimated 1,500,000 Uniate Catholics in Rumania, and about 1,200,000 of the Latin Rite. The launching of the attack to bring the members of the Uniate Church under the Russian Orthodox Church began with a bombardment of propaganda. The Pope was attacked as an ally of the Western powers, and the leaders of the Orthodox Church urged the faithful of the Uniate Churches to return to the National Church.[73]

In the summer of 1948 a number of laws were enacted by the

---

[72] Cf. *supra*, pp. 25-27.
[73] Cianfarra, *op. cit.*, p. 104.

State which were designed to cripple the operation of the Church. Ecclesiastical property was confiscated; schools were taken over by the government, and a special bureau was established "to regulate religious cult."[74] This bureau demanded that all religious organizations had to be approved by the Soviet of the National Assembly before they would be permitted to function. Moreover, the Minister of Cults was given authority to overrule any decision of the ecclesiastical authorities. The dioceses of Rumania were reduced from ten to four. The Latin Rite was given two, and the Eastern Rite was given the same number. Seven of the eleven bishops were deposed.[75]

The final phase of separating the Oriental Catholics from Rome got under way in September of 1948. The Government organized a group of officials who approached every priest of the Eastern Rite to sign a document stating that he was thereby delegating two unspecified priests to represent him at a national convention to be held in October. At this meeting the "decision" of the Oriental clergy to separate from Rome was to be announced. Some of the signatures were secured by false promises, others by means of threats of arrest and reprisals. Many who refused were deported to Siberia.[76]

On October 1st, the Congress was held and it was announced that the clergy of the Oriental Church had decided to break with Rome and return to the Orthodox Church. Despite the protests of the Oriental bishops and the Nuncio of the Holy See, Archbishop Gerald O'Hara, on December 1st, the State officially declared that the Oriental Catholic Church was illegal.[77]

On September 17, 1951, the Sacred Consistorial Congregation issued a decree declaring that those who had impeded the exercise of ecclesiastical jurisdiction in Rumania had contracted the excommunication specially reserved to the Holy See—according to canons 2343, § 3; 2334, 2°; and 2209, §§ 1, 3—and have incurred the other penalties proportionate to the quality of the delinquents, according to the Sacred Canons of the Code of Canon Law.[78]

---

[74] *Ibid.*, p. 105.

[75] *Ibid.*, p. 108.

[76] *Ibid.*, p. 109.

[77] *Ibid.*, p. 111.

[78] *AAS*, XXXXIII (1951), 603; *Digest*, III, 661-662.

The government also attempted to organize a "national" Church for the Latin Rite. The State initiated a Schismatic movement and placed at its head a priest by the name of Andreas Agotha, who was supported by a number of other priests. This group signed a resolution advocating the union of the Catholic Church with the Communist Government. It then drew up what appeared to be a harmless appeal for the outlawing of atomic weapons by the countries of the world. The Soviet Union was, at that time, advocating such control, and the local Parties, as usual, quickly got behind Moscow. This appeal was circulated among the clergy of Rumania for their signatures. A number of priests, not realizing the political implications of the petition, unwittingly ascribed to it. They soon found, however, their names appearing in the press as having favored the union of the Church with the existing government. The Communist press said that the signing of the petition to outlaw atomic weapons implicitly contained the desire to separate from Rome.[79]

Andreas Agotha, the leader of the Schismatic group, was declared *excommunicatus vitandus* by a decree of the Holy Office issued on May 2, 1950.[80]

In Czecho-Slovakia, the Communists attempted to separate the clergy and the faithful from their bishops, and eventually from Rome, by means of an organization called "Catholic Action." The facts concerning the movement have been provided by Theodorik Zubek, a Franciscan priest and former professor of Theology at the Franciscan Seminary in Zilina, Slovakia. Since his escape from a concentration camp in 1951, he has written a number of articles on the problems of the Church behind the Iron Curtain and has recently published a book dealing with the persecution of the Church in Slovakia.[81]

On June 10, 1949, the Communist authorities in Czecho-Slovakia invited, expenses paid, a number of laymen and priests to attend a meeting in Prague. All those invited were known to be disposed

[79] Cianfarra, *op. cit.*, pp. 116-117.

[80] Appeared in *L'Osservatore Romano* (Città del Vaticano, Sept. 5, 1849-May 27, 1852; July 1, 1861—), 4 May, 1950; *Digest*, III, pp. 659-660.

[81] *The Church of Silence in Slovakia* (Whiting: J. J. Lach, 1956). Cf also Galter, *The Red Book of the Persecuted Church*, chap. 12.

to directions from the Party, although they were not actually organized in the Party. At the meeting a program was adopted allegedly designed to bring about a better agreement between the Church and State and to promote a greater loyalty among the Catholic people to Czecho-Slovakia. The real purpose of the program, however, was to separate the clergy and the faithful from their bishops and Rome.[82]

The faithful, in many cases, were forced to support the group by signing their names to lists placed in shops and offices and social gatherings.[83] The Communists published not only these names, but the names of people taken from attendance cards at social gatherings, etc. They also published fictitious names, as well as the names of deceased priests. In all they gathered about 1,100 names. But the Party stated that this was clear proof that the "lower clergy" and the faithful supported the Government.[84] In actual fact, however, only a small percentage of those signing this so-called "Catholic Action Manifesto" fully understood and supported the movement.

On July 15, 1949, the bishops of Czecho-Slovakia held a joint meeting. The session resulted in the publication of a pastoral letter signed by Archbishop Beran in which the "Catholic Action" organized by the Communists was branded as an anti-ecclesiastical, schismatical movement, and hence no Catholic was to take part in it. The pastoral letter was to be read at the Masses on Sunday, June 19th. Despite attempts made by the police to prevent this message from reaching the people, many of the priests did read it to the faithful on the appointed day. On the following day, June 20th, the Holy Office issued a decree in which it reprobated and condemned as schismatical the action fraudulently called "Catholic

[82] T. Zubek, "Dissolving of the Church Organization in the Countries Behind the 'Iron Curtain,'" *The Homiletic and Pastoral Review* (New York, 1900—), LV (1955), 107.

[83] Zubek, "The Latest Communistic Tactics in Fighting the Catholic Church," *The Homiletic and Pastoral Review,* LIV (1954), 405.

[84] This term "lower clergy" is a technical term used by the Party to designate the priestly proletariat. It is used to bring about a cleavage between the ordinary priests and the hierarchy. Cf. Zubek, *The Church of Silence in Slovakia,* p. 75.

Action." At the same time the Holy Office declared that all persons, clerical or lay, who knowingly and of their own accord adhered to it, or who shall do so in the future, have incurred or shall incur *ipso facto* as schismatics and apostates from the Catholic Church, the excommunication specially reserved to the Holy See, which is mentioned in canon 2314.[85]

The action taken by the bishops of Czecho-Slovakia, as well as the action taken by the Holy See, completely destroyed the usefulness of the "Catholic Action."[86]

Realizing its attempt to divide the Church in Czecho-Slovakia had failed, the Party then set into operation another technique it had used with great success in other areas. The Party gradually infiltrated into the administration of the Church on the diocesan level. The bishops were confined to their residences and the Government placed lay commissaries in the chanceries to take over the administration of the dioceses.[87] These commissaries censored all the mail and all official papers had to be cleared by them. Moreover, they acquainted themselves with the secret files of the chanceries. Although the bishops sent a letter of protest to the Government, these commissaries were not removed until the following plan was well under way.

In the spring of 1950 the Communists began to penetrate more deeply into the chanceries and the administration of the dioceses. They imprisoned chancellors, secretaries and almost all clerical employees of the chanceries who did not express a willingness to cooperate with the State Agency for Ecclesiastical Affairs.[88] The vacated positions were then filled by members of the "Patriotic Priests" organization.[89] In time, only two vicars general were not removed by the government authorities, and these two were advanced in years. Zubek notes that such a situation caused great confusion, since it was difficult to determine the validity of acts performed by these so-called officials. Some of the bishops subse-

[85] *AAS,* XXXI (1949), 333; *Digest,* III, 657-658.

[86] Zubek, *The Church of Silence in Slovakia,* p. 78.

[87] Zubek, "Dissolving of the Church Organization Behind the 'Iron Curtain,'" *The Homiletic and Pastoral Review,* LV (1955), 110.

[88] Zubek, *The Church of Silence in Slovakia,* p. 268.

[89] Cf. *supra,* pp. 27-28 concerning "Patriotic Priests."

quently approved these State-appointed men; others did not. Zubek is of the opinion that this terrible state of affairs might have been one of the reasons that provoked six of the bishops of Czecho-Slovakia to take the oath of loyalty to the State on March 12, 1951. Zubek says:

> It is difficult to understand this act of the ordinaries. The isolation and severance from the world in which the Communists had kept the bishops for almost a year, certainly had something to do with it. At the same time, the Communists no doubt exerted pressure on the bishops, as the Reds do so well. . . . It is certain that when the bishops took the oath of loyalty, their intentions were good—to rescue what could be rescued of the structure of the Church. They attempted to get back into their hands the helm of the dioceses which were seized from them and which a wild current threatened to carry away. Or perhaps they at least hoped to gain time for evaluation of further developments.[90]

In connection with this technique of the Communist Party behind the Iron Curtain, that is, the appointing of ecclesiastical offices, it is well to note the provisions of a decree issued by the Holy Office in 1950. This decree, issued on June 29th of that year provided that an excommunication specially reserved to the Holy See is *ipso facto* incurred by those who contrive against legitimate ecclesiastical authorities or who attempt in any way to subvert their authority. The decree also states the penalty is incurred by those who, without a canonical investiture or provision made according to the sacred canons, occupy an ecclesiastical office or benefice or dignity, or allow anyone to be unlawfully intruded into the same, or who retains the same, or who have any part directly or indirectly in these crimes.[91]

Zubek sums up the problems facing the Church in countries behind the Iron Curtain in this way:

> . . . The Communists have made great inroads into the organization of the Church. In dealing with the Com-

[90] *The Church of Silence in Slovakia,* p. 280.
[91] *AAS,* XXXXII (1950), 601; *Digest,* III, 69-71.

munists, it is always a problem to decide how far one may go without being in conflict with the divine laws, those of the Church and the conscience of man. Through concessions, spiritual strength is sapped and weakened so that, when the last phase of the struggle comes, who knows whether there will still be the power of resistance. In compromising with the Communists, the honorable side has always suffered. To the Communists, the success of their cause is the norm of morality, not divine laws or conscience; they do not consider themselves bound by any given word.

The measures of the Communist regime, repeated use of instruments of terror and convincing, brutality and trickery, power and fraud, bribery and demoralization had their influence on all classes of the inhabitants, and to a certain degree on the clergy.[92]

---

[92] *The Church of Silence in Slovakia*, pp. 298-299.

PART II

Canonical Commentary

CHAPTER III

The Status of Communists Under the Laws of the Church

INTRODUCTION

Judging from the present condition of world affairs, it is not presumptuous to say that Communism will be a pressing problem for some time to come. Nor is it pessimistic to predict that the Communist Party by its clever tactics and strategy will continue to attract, or force, portions of the faithful to its ranks as it has already done, despite the numerous condemnations of Communism made by the Church over the past one hundred years.

Accordingly, the present chapter, The Status of Communists Under the Laws of the Church, investigates the canonico-juridical position of those who associate themselves with the Communist movement in one of three ways: by professing the errors of Communism; by merely joining the Communist Party; or by showing favor to the movement in some way. The reason for including all three groups under the term "Communist" has already been stated.[1]

ARTICLE 1. THOSE WHO PROFESS THE DOCTRINES OF COMMUNISM

The question of determining the canonico-juridical status of the faithful who profess the doctrines of Communism has never presented any real problem. The philosophy of Communism is materialistic; it denies revelation, the immortality of the soul, freedom of the will, the existence of God, and the basic rights of man. In a word, it is totally opposed to Christianity. Consequently, any Catholic who would accept such a philosophy must be classified as an apostate from the faith. Even the pre-Code authors,[2] treating

---

[1] Cf. *supra*, p. vii.

[2] E.g. Genicot, *Institutiones Theologiae Moralis* (6. ed. recognita et aucta J. Salamans, 2 vols., Bruxellis, 1909), II, 623; Lehmkuhl, *Theologia Moralis* (12. ed., 2 vols., Friburgi Brisgoviae, 1914), II, 703; Noldin, *De Poenis Ecclesiasticis* (5. ed., Oeniponte, 1905), p. 65.

the question of those who profess the doctrines of Communism, placed such under the first article of the Constitution *Apostolicae Sedis.* This article of the Constitution (1869) provided an *ipso facto* excommunication specially reserved to the Holy See for all those who were guilty of the crimes of apostasy, heresy, and schism.[3]

The Decree of the Holy Office on Communists issued in 1949 confirmed this traditional stand on those who profess the doctrines of Communism. Question n. 4 of this Decree reads as follows:

> Whether the faithful who profess the materialistic and anti-Christian doctrine of Communists, and especially those who defend or propagate it, incur *ipso facto* as apostates from the Catholic faith the excommunication specially reserved to the Holy See.

The reply of the Holy Office was in the affirmative.[4]

There is no doubt then that a Catholic who professes Communism commits the crime which canon 2314[5] punishes by an excommunication specially reserved to the Holy See.[6] However, since canon 2228 ordains that the penalty determined by law is not incurred unless the crime be perfectly consummated according to the strict wording of the law, it is necessary to determine what the delict of apostasy comprehends.

Section I. The Delict of Apostasy

Apostasy is defined in canon 1325, § 2 as total rejection of the Christian faith by one who has received baptism.[7]

---

[3] Pius IX, const. *Apostolicae Sedis,* 12 Oct. 1869—*Fontes,* III, n. 552.

[4] *AAS,* XXXXI (1949), 334; *Digest,* III, 658-659.

[5] *Codex Iuris Canonici Pii X Pontificis Maximi iussu digestus Benedicti Papae XV auctoritate promulgatus, Praefatione, Fontium Annotatione et Indice Analytico-Alphabetico ab Emo Petro Card. Gasparri Auctus* (Romae: Typis Polyglottis, Vaticanis, 1917; reimpressio, 1934).

[6] Canon 2314, § 1: "Omnes a christiana fide apostatae et omnes et singuli haeretici aut schismatici: 1° Incurrunt ipso facto excommunicationem . . ."; the reservation is treated in § 2 of this canon.

[7] Canon 1325, § 2: "Post baptismum . . . si a fide christiana totaliter recedit, apostata. . . ."

A) Baptism

The first point to note concerning the delict of apostasy is that the individual must have been baptized. A catechumen, therefore, who accepts all the teachings of the Church but returns to infidelity before he receives baptism does not commit the delict of apostasy. It is only through baptism that a person becomes directly subject to the Church, and hence liable to Her punishments.[8] Moreover, it is only through baptism of water (*baptismum fluminis*) that the indelible character is received and the ecclesiastical personality. Baptism of desire or baptism of blood produce the theological effects received by baptism of water, but they do not produce its juridic effects.[9] Hence, baptism of water is the prime requisite in this consideration of the delict of apostasy.

Furthermore, the authors who comment on the words *"a fide christiana"* of canon 1325 understand Christian faith to mean the true Catholic faith. Hence, one who had been baptized and reared in an heretical sect, and later embraced atheism would not be considered an apostate, strictly speaking.[10]

---

[8] Canons 12 and 87. Suarez said that such a person, that is a catechumen who abandons the faith, theologically speaking can be described as an apostate, but he could not incur the penalties of the Church since he is not directly subject to Her jurisdiction.—*Opera Omnia* (vivès editio, ed. Carolus Berton, 26 vols., Parisiis, 1856-1861), XXIII, *de censuris,* disp. XXI, sect. II, 507.

[9] Cf. canon 737.

[10] Cf. Cipollini, *De Censuris Latae Sententiae Iuxta Codicem Iuris Canonici* (Taurini: Marietti, 1925), p. 96; Regatillo, *Institutiones Iuris Canonici* (4. ed., 2 vols., Santander: Sal Terrae, 1951), II, 535; Noldin, H.-Schmitt, A., *Summa Theologiae Moralis* (3 vols., Vol. II, 27. ed., Oeniponte: Typis et Sumptibus Fel. Rauch, 1941), II, 28. However, as Woywod notes: "As to heresy, it may be noted that formal heresy only is punished in canon 2314; wherefore . . . persons who were born and educated in an heretical sect, and never knew the true Faith, cannot be said to have stubbornly denied or rejected the Catholic Faith, and thus do not incur the penalties of canon 2314. Nevertheless, in the external forum they are not free from the penalties of canon 2314, for, in accordance with canon 2200, when there is the external violation of a law of the Church, malice is presumed in the external forum until its absence is proved."—*A Practical Commentary on The Code of Canon Law* (2 vols., New York: Joseph F. Wagner, Inc., 1925), II, 466. Cf. also instruction of 1859 regarding reception of converts,—*Fontes,* IV, n. 953.

B) Total Defection

The second essential feature of the crime of apostasy, according to the definition provided by canon 1325, is that the person must totally reject the faith. Apostasy is distinguished from heresy inasmuch as the heretic does not reject all the dogmas but only one or some. However, heresy and apostasy are not specifically distinct sins, and both are subject to the same penalties.[11] Laymann described the difference between apostasy and heresy as merely a difference of degress.[12]

Moreover, this total rejection of the faith must be deliberate and voluntary, or as Coronata describes it, "*interne seu animo.*"[13] In the words of the pre-Code authors, the sin of apostasy must be true and formal, not merely material and objective.[14] The authors also note that what are commonly called "indifferent Catholics," or those who ordinarily neglect their religious obligations are not necessarily apostates. Frequently, such people lack a real internal desire (*animus*) to separate themselves from the faith.[15]

C) Externally Manifested

Although the deliberate and voluntary decision to abandon the faith is sufficient to constitute the sin of apostasy, it is not delictual until the person in some way manifests this choice externally. This follows from the very nature of an ecclesiastical crime, that is, it must be an *external* violation of the law.[16] A delict, it must be

---

[11] MacKenzie, *The Delict of Heresy in Its Commission, Penalization, Absolution,* The Catholic University of America Canon Law Studies, n. 77 (Washington, D. C.: The Catholic University of America, 1932), p. 17 (hereafter cited as MacKenzie).

[12] *Theologia Moralis* (2 vols. in 1, Venetiis, 1630), Lib. II, Tract 1, cap. XVI, p. 213.

[13] *Institutiones Iuris Canonici* (5 vols., Taurini-Romae: Marietti, Vols. I-III, 2. ed., 1939-1941; Vol. IV, 4. ed., 1955; Vol. V, 3. ed., 1951), IV, 290 (hereafter cited as *Institutiones*).

[14] Pirhing, *Ius Canonicum Nova Methodo Explicatum* (5 vols., in 4, Dilignae, 1674-1678), Lib. V, tit. VII, 112.

[15] Coronata, *op. cit.*, p. 291; cf. *infra*, pp. 76-80.

[16] Canon 2195: "Nomine delicti, iure ecclesiastico, intelligitur externa et moraliter imputabilis legis violatio cui addita sit sanctio canonica saltem indeterminata."

remembered, is not only a moral violation, it is also a sinful disturbance of the social order. But this *damnum sociale* is not found in internal sins. To state this principle more graphically, should a person sit down in the quiet of his room, and having read Marx, Engels, and Stalin, decide to abandon the faith and accept atheistic Communism, unless he manifests this choice externally, he has not committed the delict of professing Communism and hence not the delict of apostasy.

This external manifestation can be made in any number of ways, by speech, by the written word, or even by actions. Nor must this external manifestation be made in a public manner; an occult external manifestation, witnessed by no one is sufficient. To return to the man who decides, in the quiet of his room, to reject the faith and accept the philosophy of Communism, should he, for example, vocalize this decision, even though no one heard him, this act would be sufficient to incur the penalty. Pirhing explains the reason for this conclusion by pointing out that such a deed is not *per se* occult, since by its very nature it can stand before the Church and be judged. It is in the external forum, subject to the jurisdiction of the Church. It is only *per accidens* occult because there were no witnesses present when the crime was committed.[17] Reiffenstuel phrases this concept in a different way. He states that an occult act which no one witnessed can be considered a sufficient externalization of a man's mind, because the act by its very nature is cognizable and subject to the jurisdiction of the Church.[18]

Moreover, this external act by which the internal sin of apostasy is manifested must be performed as a profession or assertion accepting apostasy.[19] The penalty is incurred for the external sin of apostasy only when the latter is formed by the internal sin of apostasy and proceeds from it. Pirhing cites the example of a man who goes to another and manifests his internal sin of apostasy, but he does so for the sake of advice or instruction. This act would not incur the penalty since it was not the declaration or

---

[17] *Op. cit.*, Lib. V, Tit. VII, p. 113.

[18] *Ius Canonicum Universum* (5 vols. in 7, Parisiis: 1864-1870), VII, Lib. V, n. 236.

[19] Canon 2200.

assertion accepting the apostasy.[20] The same would hold true for the man who confesses the internal sin of apostasy in the sacrament of penance.[21]

Somewhat more complicated is the case of the Catholic who externally gives manifestation of abandoning the faith but interiorly he retains his belief in the Church. This could readily occur during persecutions. It is the teaching of canonists that such a one, although in the internal forum is not a true apostate, in the external forum the person has professed apostasy and therefore he has made himself liable to the punishments inflicted on this crime.[22] The presumption is that the person's actions bespeak his mind.[23]

It was stated before that Catholics who fail to perform their religious obligations, even for a long period of time, are not thereby to be considered apostates.[24] But this should not be taken as an absolute rule, for as Kerin notes, Catholics who fail to perform their religious obligations in certain circumstances probably can be interpreted as professing their internal sin of apostasy.[25] He bases this conclusion on canon 1325, § 1, which states that the faithful of Christ are obliged to profess their faith openly whenever their silence, backwardness, or manner of acting would involve an implicit denial of the faith, contempt of religion, an offense to God, or scandal to the neighbor. The law, therefore, permits an

---

[20] *Op. cit.*, Lib. V, Tit. VII, p. 113.

[21] MacKenzie, pp. 33-34.

[22] Schmalzgrueber: "Quando quis verbis tantum, aut factis, non tamen animo descisit a fide Catholica, et hic probabilius in foro conscientiae non afficitur excommunicatione, aut aliis apostatarum poenis; quia haereticus aut apostata nemo est, nisi qui scienter, et sponte animo a fide, et religione Catholica discedit. In foro tamen exteriori censetur apostata . . . et punitur ab Ecclesia, utpote quae probabiliter credit, eum mente, et animo recessisse a fide."—*Ius Ecclesiasticum Universum* (5 vols. in 12, Romae, 1843-1845), Vol. V, Pars Prima, Tit. IX *de apostatis,* p. 362; cf. also Reiffenstuel, *op. cit.*, VI, Tit. V, n. 234.

[23] Canon 2200, § 2.

[24] Cf. *supra,* p. 74.

[25] *The Privation of Christian Burial,* The Catholic University of America Canon Law Studies, n. 136 (Washington, D. C.: The Catholic University of America Press, 1941), pp. 165-166.

implication of apostasy to arise from circumstances. In Kerin's words, "The failure to respond to the demands of the law will permit the implication of the denial of the faith to stand as a warranted assumption."[26] In other words, if in a given set of circumstances an individual's neglect of those religious duties that are so strongly binding on all the faithful, v.g. Sunday Mass, "Easter Duty," etc., may properly be viewed by the community as the external manifestation of the person's interior abandonment of the faith, the individual has then and there an obligation to give some external manifestation of his faith. Otherwise, he permits "the implication of the denial to stand as a warranted assumption."[27] The circumstances alone, however, can determine when and where and how such neglect will be considered as a denial of the faith. Consequently, in a community where the practice of the faith is widely neglected, it is not likely that one's neglect of so basic an obligation as attendance at Sunday Mass would be looked upon by the community as the result of the person's rejection of the faith.[28]

Perhaps a practical example will better illustrate the principle. It was seen in the first chapter[29] that in many countries behind the Iron Curtain, the governments permit the Church to function on a limited scale. Mass on Sunday and the administration of the sacraments is tolerated. Despite these conditions, or perhaps because of them, the faith is stronger and more manifest than ever before. At the same time, in many areas the faithful are obliged to enroll in the Communist Party. Surely, however, this is not looked upon by the faithful as an indication of abandonment of the faith.[30] But suppose, for the sake of example, that a Catholic in a small village behind the Iron Curtain is constrained to join the Party along with the other members of his community. But

---

[26] *Op. cit.*, p. 166.

[27] *Loc. cit.*

[28] *Loc. cit.*

[29] *Supra*, pp. 26-28.

[30] It is to be noted that the Decree of the Holy Office issued in 1949 said that it was unlawful to give the sacraments to those who *knowingly* and *willingly* joined the Communist Party.—*AAS*, XXXXI (1949), p. 334 (italics inserted); *Digest*, III, 658.

this particular person begins to read the Communist literature and take seriously the ever-present Communist propaganda. In the course of time he interiorly abandons the faith. As yet, he has not committed the delict of apostasy. Before long, however, he neglects to fulfill the religious obligations which the other members of the community are consistently satisfying. In such circumstances it is quite possible for the people to consider his conduct the result of an abandonment of the faith. In such cases there could even be a serious obligation to make an open profession of the faith to avoid giving scandal to one's neighbor.[31]

Question n. 4 of the Decree of the Holy Office issued in 1949 asked whether the faithful who profess the materialistic and anti-Christian doctrines of Communists, and especially those who defend and propagate it, incur *ipso facto* as apostates from the Catholic faith the excommunication especially reserved to the Holy See.[32] Lest these words *defend* and *propagate* be confused with the provisions of canon 2316, some consideration must be given to that canon. The portion of this canon which is of interest here is the first part which states that anyone who knowingly and freely assists in any way in the propagation of heresy is himself suspected of heresy.[33]

This canon primarily deals with those actions which in some way are assisting in the propagation of heresy. But these actions in themselves do not clearly and unmistakably indicate that the individual has accepted the heretical doctrine. Rather, the actions are such that they throw suspicion on his state of mind. It is a suspicion based on evidence which does not afford conclusive proof that the person has actually committed the delict described in canon 2314.[34]

Suspicion is generally divided into light, vehement, and what is called violent. Light suspicion is based on absolutely insufficient evidence, and hence amounts to rash judgment. Vehement suspicion rests on effective signs and conclusions. Violent suspicion is equal to morally certain proof.[35]

---

[31] Canon 1325.

[32] *AAS*, XXXXI (1949), 334; cf. *Digest*, III, 658-659.

[33] Canon 2316.

[34] Coronata, *op. cit.*, p. 309.

[35] *Loc. cit.*

Canon 2316, therefore, must be concerned with vehement suspicion—suspicion based on facts which in themselves do not provide clear-cut evidence that the person is guilty of the delicts outlined in canon 2314, § 1. For that reason the words *defend* or *propagate* used in the Decree of the Holy Office mentioned above are not referring to those actions that merely constitute vehement suspicion. They must refer to actions that in themselves clearly manifest that the person has interiorly accepted the doctrines of Communism. The phrasing of the Decree, "the faithful who profess the materialistic and anti-Christian doctrine of Communists, especially those who defend and propagate it . . ." leaves no other conclusion. Defense and propagation in this context must be considered as aggravated profession, a manifestation and self-confession.

By way of example, two men, *A* and *B* are members of the Communist Party in a country where membership itself is not considered as an external manifestation of accepting the Communist doctrine. *A* has entirely abandoned the faith and has become a devoted Party man. He gives lectures on Communism, and writes articles for the Communist press. He is active in all the Party's activities, and freely contributes his time and money to defend and propagate Communism. *A* obviously falls under canon 2314, § 1.

B, the other Party member, is far from being a devout Catholic, but occasionally he does fulfill his religious obligations. However, he is occasionally seen at the Party meetings; he pays his dues, and subscribes to the Party paper. He has been heard to praise the efforts of the Communist leaders and the work the Party is doing. Nor is he loathe to associate with the leading Communists. In short, he has not performed actions which in themselves clearly amount to a profession of Communism. Hence, in view of the considerations above, *B* would not fall under canon 2314. Nevertheless, his actions, associating with heretics, praising their methods and objectives, giving them material support have traditionally been considered as aiding in the propagation of heresy.[86] Therefore, canon 2315 can be applied to *B*. This canon provides that the proper authority should warn such an individual to remove the causes of suspicion.[87] If the warning proves fruitless, the suspected person must be forbidden to perform any ecclesiastical legal acts, according to canon 2256. If he is a cleric, he must be suspended *a divinis,* after a second warning has been left unheeded. If within six months the person has not removed the suspicion, he must be regarded as a heretic and subject to the penalties of canon 2314.

Because of the nature of circumstantial evidence upon which suspicions are based, no hard and fast rule can be set down to distinguish violent suspicion from vehement suspicion. Each case must be examined and judged in the light of the circumstances of time and place, keeping in mind that violent suspicion is equivalent to moral certitude.

D) Excusing Causes

It is not the purpose of this work to present an exhaustive treatment of all the causes excusing one from the penalty imposed by the law on those professing Communism. However, it will be necessary to consider those which most frequently come into play in the question of association with the Communist movement. They are: ignorance, force, and fear.[88]

---

[86] Under the pre-Code Constitution *Apostolicae Sedis,* the following incurred an excommunication especially reserved to the Holy See: "Omnes a christiana fide apostatas, et omnes ac singulos haereticos, quocumque nomine censeantur, et cuiuscumque sectae existant, eisque credentes, eorumque receptores, fautores, ac generaliter quoslibet illorum defensores."—*Fontes,* III, n. 552. The pre-Code authors who comment on this section of the Constitution include the actions that *B* performed under the term *fautores*. Commentators on the present Code, e.g. Coronata, *op. cit.,* pp. 309-310, understand these terms to be included in canon 2316 under the phrase "Qui quoquo modo. . . ."

[87] The warning should be given in accordance with canon 2307.

[88] For a complete treatment of these excusing causes, see Swobada, *Ignorance in Relation to the Imputability of Delicts,* The Catholic University of America Canon Law Studies, n. 143 (Washington, D. C.: The Catholic University of America Press, 1941); McGrath, *Comparative Study of Crime and Its Imputability in Ecclesiastical Criminal Law, and in Amer-*

Basic in this whole consideration of delicts and penalties is canon 2218, § 2, which provides that those circumstances which excuse from all imputability as well as those which excuse from grievous sin also render the person immune from every penalty *latae* as well as *ferendae sententiae,* even in the external forum, provided the excusing causes can be proven in the external forum.[39] Hence, if a person has committed a delict, for example, professing Communism, unless he has committed a mortal sin, he has not incurred the penalty in the internal forum. However, as far as the person's canonico-juridical status is concerned, he is considered under the penalty unless the causes that excused from sin can be proved in the external forum. It must be remembered that a person's canonico-juridical status can only be determined from external data, that is, what is cognizable by the Church.[40]

In addition to committing a grave violation of the law, since the crime of professing Communism is punished by a censure, the delinquent must act with contumacy.[41] In general, contumacy signifies a defiance of the law. But in penal matters contumacy denotes a disobedience of a specific nature, since it is a type of disobedience implying contempt for authority.[42] This contempt of authority, however, need not be formal or express; virtual contempt is sufficient. For that reason, the law demands a canonical admonition before a *ferendae sententiae* censure can be inflicted.[43] In the case of *latae sententiae* censures the law stating that the

---

ican Criminal Law, The Catholic University of America Canon Law Studies, n. 385 (Washington, D. C.: The Catholic University of America Press, 1957); McCoy, *Force and Fear in Relation to Delictual Imputability and Penal Responsibility,* The Catholic University of America Canon Law Studies, n. 200 (Washington, D. C.: The Catholic University of America Press, 1944).

[39] Canon 2200, § 2 states that once the law has been externally violated, *dolus* is presumed until the contrary is proven.

[40] Hence, the famous dictum: "De internis non iudicat Ecclesia." This problem is discussed again under the canonical effects of the delict of professing Communism, cf. *infra,* pp. 146-156.

[41] Canon 2242, § 1: "Censura punitur tantummodo delictum externum, grave, consummatum, cum contumacia coniunctum. . . ."

[42] Swobada, *op. cit.,* p. 171.

[43] Canon 2242, § 2.

particular penalty is to be incurred *ipso facto* for the violation of the law is considered by the law as sufficient admonition. This is explicitly stated in canon 2242, § 2:

> . . . ad incurrendam vero censuram latae sententiae sufficit transgressio legis vel praecepti cui sit adnexa latae sententiae poena, nisi reus legitima causa ab hac excusetur.

The canon just quoted, it will be noticed, says that the delinquent incurs the penalty *"nisi reus legitima causa ab hac excusetur."* In order to determine what causes excuse the delinquent from incurring the penalty, recourse must be had to canons 2199 to 2206, and canon 2229. Although there are a number of excusing causes mentioned in these canons, only three will be considered here: ignorance, force and fear.

Ignorance. Ignorance, as defined by St. Thomas, is the privation of knowledge in a subject naturally capable of and constituted for knowledge.[44] Affected ignorance is a directly voluntary lack of obligatory knowledge which ignorance is procured by a positive effort and from a wrongful motive.[45] Crass or supine ignorance is a form of ignorance that results from a complete lack of diligence when it is known that the truth could easily be discovered.[46] If there is not a complete lack of ignorance, only partial, or the truth is not *easily* discoverable, provided there is sufficient culpability for the commission of a mortal sin, then the ignorance is grave.[47]

Another important distinction is that between ignorance of the law and ignorance of fact. If the existence, extent or meaning of the law is not known, there is present ignorance of the law. If the concrete or physical conditions necessary for the application of the law are not known there is ignorance of fact.[48]

Having set forth the various types of ignorance, it now remains to determine which will excuse from the penalty of excommunication imposed on those who profess Communism.[49]

---

[44] *Summa Theologica* (5 vols., Taurini: Marietti, 1938), I-II, q. 76, art. 2.
[45] Swobada, *op. cit.*, p. 140.
[46] *Ibid.*, p. 151.
[47] *Loc. cit.*
[48] *Loc. cit.*
[49] That is, those who fall under canon 2314.

Canon 2229, § 3 says that if the law does not demand perfect *dolus*, then crass or supine ignorance will not excuse from the penalty. A law demanding perfect *dolus* is one which contains such words as: *praesumpserit, ausus fuerit, scienter, studiose, temerarie, consulto egerit*, or other similar words which indicate that full knowledge and deliberation are required.[50] Now, canon 2314, the canon which contains the penalty for the crime of apostasy, gives no indication that perfect *dolus* is required in the commission of the crime of apostasy. Moreover, canon 1325, the canon which defines the sin of apostasy, merely states: "*Post receptum baptismum . . . si a fide christiana totaliter recedit, apostata. . . .*" It is true that in the same canon the lawmaker, in defining heresy, employs the word *pertinaciter*. However, there seems to be no justification for reading *pertinaciter* in the clause defining apostasy. Although it is generally agreed that apostasy and heresy are not specifically distinct sins, they are, nevertheless, looked upon by the law as distinct crimes.

Therefore, it seems that perfect *dolus*, although demanded in the crime of heresy, is not demanded in the crime of apostasy.[51] Hence, ignorance which is crass or supine will not excuse.[52] Only mere grave and venial ignorance will excuse from the penalty.[53] Grave ignorance is midway between crass and venial ignorance. If some diligence has been used, but it falls short of the measure which a prudent man would use under the facts and circumstances, then the ignorance is grave. Otherwise it is venial.[54] Naturally, affected ignorance can never be offered as an excusing cause.[55]

Briefly, then, mere grave ignorance of the law, the fact, or the penalty imposed for the violation of the law, will excuse from the excommunication incurred for the crime of professing Communism. Affected, crass or supine ignorance will not excuse.

---

[50] Canon 2229, § 2.

[51] Generally, the authors do not treat this specific point.

[52] Canon 2229, § 3: Si lex verba illa habeat: 1° Ignorantia legis aut etiam solius poenae, si fuerit crassa vel supina, a nulla poena latae sententiae eximit. . . ."

[53] Canon 2229, § 3, 1°.

[54] Swobada, *op. cit.*, p. 138.

[55] Canon 2229, § 1.

Fear. Since the crime of apostasy involves a contempt of faith, then fear, even grave fear, cannot be offered as an excusing cause.[56] The same can be said for grave necessity and grave hardship since they are parallel to grave fear.[57]

Force. Canon 2205, § 1, states that absolute physical force which deprives a man of all freedom of action absolutely excuses from imputability, or in other words entirely precludes a delict. This principle really needs no explanation or proof, for an act which is performed in consequence of absolute force, when one's will is positively set against the performance of the act, strictly considered is the act of the one who perpetrates the force.[58]

The wording of canon 2205, § 1, clearly requires absolute force for the complete preclusion of a delict. Absolute force is one that entirely deprives the person of all freedom of action, or as it is stated in canon 103, § 1, "an external force which cannot be resisted." If the force can be resisted, if there is some freedom of action, then the force is called moderate (*vis modica*). As an excusing cause this moderate force can be classified as a necessity or hardship, grave or slight according to the nature of the force. Now, since grave necessity and grave hardship are placed in the same category as grave fear,[59] it follows then that these cannot be offered as excusing causes for the commission of the crime of professing Communism (apostasy) inasmuch as this crime involves a contempt of faith. And grave fear, or what is equal to grave fear, will not be admitted.[60]

Therefore, by way of summary, one who externally, even occultly, professes the doctrines of Communism, and especially one who defends or propagates these doctrines, incurs an excommunication specially reserved to the Holy See.[61] It is worth noting, too,

---

[56] Canon 2229, § 3, 3°: "Metus gravis, si delictum vergat in contemptum fidei aut ecclesiasticae auctoritatis vel in publicum animarum damnum, a poenis latae sententiae nullatenus eximit."

[57] Canon 2205, §§ 2 and 3; cf. McCoy, *op. cit.*, p. 130.

[58] McCoy, *op. cit.*, p. 87.

[59] Canon 2205, § 2.

[60] Canon 2205, § 3; canon 2229, § 3, 3°; cf. also McCoy, *op. cit.*, p. 130.

[61] Canon 2314. If a person defends or propagates a movement, he is to be in law presumed thereby to admit and profess it; cf. canon 2200, § 2.

that a person can be guilty of the crime of professing Communism, and yet never be affiliated with the Communist Party. It was seen in the first chapter[62] that there are a number of people who never join the Communist Party, nor in any way under its direction, but still they knowingly and freely support the Communist movement in one way or another.

ARTICLE 2. THOSE WHO JOIN THE COMMUNIST PARTY

Section I. The Crime of Joining the Party

In the previous article it was seen that the determination of the canonico-juridical status of a person who professes Communism has never presented any great problem. Traditionally, such a person has been considered an apostate and hence subject to the penalty provided for that crime, namely, excommunication.[63] Moreover, the Decree of the Holy Office issued in 1949 has confirmed this traditional doctrine.[64]

However, determining the basic canonico-juridical status of a person who merely joins the Communist Party has never been an easy task. The question was even discussed in pre-Code days. Nor can it be said that the Decree of the Holy Office issued in 1949 has settled the question.[65]

The authors who treat the question of the *Nomen Dantes* fall into two groups. One group says that those who give their names to the Communist Party are liable to the excommunication provided in canon 2335, the canon censuring those who join the

---

[62] Cf. *supra*, pp. 38-40.

[63] Canon 2314, § 1, 1°.

[64] *AAS*, XXXXI (1949), 334; *Digest*, III, 658-659.

[65] Some commentators on the Decree of 1949 suggest that the Holy Office has confirmed the opinion that the Communist Party does not fall under canon 2335, the canon imposing excommunication on those who join the Masons and other similar sects; cf. L. McReavy, "The Holy Office on Communism," *The Clergy Review* (London: 1931-), XXXII (1949), 392-393; W. Conway, "The Decree of the Holy Office on Communism," *The Irish Ecclesiastical Record* (Dublin: 1864-; 5th Series 1913-), LXXIII (1950), 61.

Masons and other similar societies.[66] The other opinion holds that the Communist Party cannot be included under canon 2335, and therefore to join the Party, although seriously sinful, does not beget the penalty of excommunication. The authors who hold these opinions will be seen shortly.

Basically, what divides the schools of thought is the interpretation of the phrase found in canon 2335, *"eiusdem generis associationibus."* The opinion which holds that the Communist Party cannot be classified as a society similar to the Masons is following the school that says *"eiusdem generis"* means Masonic in rite, form, procedure, or at least the organization must be in some way secret. The opposite school follows the opinion that says an organization is *"eiusdem generis"* if it is machinating against the Church or the state. Secrecy is not an essential feature, according to this school.

The writer favors the latter opinion, namely, that joining any sect or society machinating against the Church or the state is subject to canon 2335. And therefore, the Communist Party, since it is machinating to overthrow the Church and the whole social order,[67] must be included under canon 2335. It then follows that merely joining the Communist Party begets the excommunication in canon 2335.

Before advancing the arguments that uphold this view, it is necessary to set forth the precise definitions of a few terms frequently used in connection with this problem. A *condemned* society is one in which the Church forbids her subjects to take membership.[68] Condemned societies, in turn, may be divided in three different ways. They may be divided according to their nature, for example, Anti-Social, Secret, Bible, Cremation, and Theosophical Societies. They may also be divided according to the manner of their condemnation. Hence, some societies are con-

---

[66] The pre-Code authors who followed this school placed the Communists under a similar law contained in the Constitution *Apostolicae Sedis—Fontes,* III, p. 27, n. 4. Canon 2335 is based on this pre-Code law.

[67] Cf. *supra,* Chapter II, *Papal Statements on Communism.*

[68] Quigley, *Condemned Societies,* The Catholic University of America Canon Law Studies, n. 46 (Washington, D. C.: The Catholic University of America, 1927), p. 7.

demned by name, *nominatim;* others are implicitly condemned. Finally, condemned societies can be divided according to the sanction attached to their condemnations. Some are condemned under censure, while others are condemned without censure, but membership is forbidden *sub gravi.*[69]

Although frequently writers will group secret societies and anti-social societies all under the term secret societies, these two different types of societies should be kept distinct.[70] Every secret society is not at the same time an anti-social society, nor is every anti-social society a secret society. An anti-social society is one which conspires or plots against the Church or the state, or both. A secret society is an organization, the members of which are bound to secrecy concerning their constitutions, purposes, means, degree work, and the like.[71]

For some time the arguments substantiating the opinion that some form of secrecy or clandestinity is essential in the notion of *"eiusdem generis"* were taken from Vermeersch.[72] In recent times an article by Ganzi, appearing in *Periodica* has been frequently cited.[73]

One argument advanced by Vermeersch, and others,[74] to demonstrate that secrecy or clandestinity is essential to the notion of *"eiusdem generis"* is the fact that it is the commonly held opinion.[75] Quigley, upholding the opposite opinion, investigated a number of authors and finds that the opinion held by Vermeersch and others is not as common as it is claimed to be. Quigley,[76] notes that of those authors who wrote before the Code, Nilles,[77]

---

[69] *Loc. cit.*

[70] *Ibid.*, p. 8.

[71] *Loc. cit.*

[72] *De Prohibitione et Censura Librorum* (2. ed., Romae: 1898), p. 62 sq.

[73] "Nomen Dantes Communismo," *Periodica,* XXXVII (1948), 102-108; as the title indicates, this article deals specifically with the problem of the Communist Party. Vermeersch treats condemned societies in general.

[74] It is implied by Conway, *art. cit.*, 60-61.

[75] Vermeersch, *op. cit.*, p. 62; cf. also Vermeersch-Creusen, *Epitome Iuris Canonici* (3 vols., Mechlinae-Romae: H. Dessain, Vol. I, 7. ed., 1949; Vol. II, 6. ed., 1940; Vol. III, 6. ed., 1946), III, 331.

[76] *Op. cit.*, p. 62.

[77] *Commentarium in Concilium Plenarium Baltimorense Tertium* (2 vols., Oeniponte: Ex Officina F. Raush, 1888), II, 308-309.

D'Annibale,[78] Sabetti,[79] Bucceroni,[80] Lehmkuhl (in his earlier editions),[81] Genicot (also in his earlier editions),[82] Bargilliat,[83] and Aertnys[84] did not hold the opinion maintained by Vermeersch.

Of the authors who have written after the Code, Quigley notes that Blat,[85] Ayrinhac,[86] Farrugia,[87] Sole,[88] Pighi,[89] Tanquerey,[90] Prummer,[91] Eichmann,[92] Cappello,[93] Cippolini,[94] and Pistocchi[95] do not agree with the opinion expressed by Vermeersch. To this list presented by Quigley, others not mentioned by him can be added. For example, Zitelli,[96] Elbel,[97] Cima,[98] De Luca,[99] Salucci,[100]

---

[78] *Summula Theologiae Moralis* (3. ed., 3 vols., Romae, 1892), I, 358, n. 4.

[79] *Compendium Theologiae Moralis* (12. ed., Neo-Eboraci et Cincinaati, 1896), p. 780.

[80] *Institutiones Theologiae Moralis* (6. ed., 4 vols., Romae, 1915), IV, 234.

[81] *Theologia Moralis* (5. ed., 2 vols., Friburgi Brisgoviae, 1888), II, p. 697.

[82] *Institutiones Theologiae Moralis* (2 vols., Lovanii, 1896), II, 762.

[83] *Praelectiones Iuris Canonici* (28. ed., 2 vols., Parisiis, 1913), II, 518.

[84] *Theologia Moralis Iuxta Doctrinam S. Alphonsi de Ligorio* (2 vols., Tornaci, 1893), II, 399.

[85] *Commentarium Textus Iuris Canonici* (5 vols. in 6, Romae: Ex Typographia Pontificia in Instituto Pii X, 1924), V, 225.

[86] *Penal Legislation in the New Code of Canon Law* (revised by P. Lydon, New York: Benziger Brothers, 1936), p. 241.

[87] *Commentarium in Censuris Latae Sententiae Codicis Iuris Canonici* (2. ed., Melitae, 1921), p. 68.

[88] *De Delictis et Poenis* (Romae: Pustet, 1920), p. 269.

[89] *Censurae Latae Sententiae et Irregularitates* (5. ed., Veronae, 1919), p. 31.

[90] *Synopsis Theologiae Moralis et Pastoralis* (7. ed., 3 vols., Romae, 1922), II, 689.

[91] *Manuale Theologiae Moralis* (3. ed., 3 vols., Friburgi Brisgoviae, 1923), III, 355.

[92] *Das Strafrecht des Codex Iuris Canonici* (Paderborn: Schoningh, 1920), pp. 150-151.

[93] *De Censuris Iuxta Codicem Iuris Canonici* (3. ed., Taurinorum Augustae: Marietti, 1933), pp. 268-269.

[94] *De Censuris Latae Sententiae*, p. 134.

[95] *Canonici Penali del Codice Ecclesiastico, Espositi e Commentati* (Torino-Romae: Marietti, 1925), p. 102.

[96] *Apparatus Iuris Ecclesiastici* (3. ed., Romae, 1903), p. 544.

[97] *Theologia Moralis Per Modum Conferentiarum* (ed. I. Bierbaum, 3 vols., Paderbornae, 1892), III, 624.

[98] *Commentario alla Costituzione Apostolicae Sedis* (Genova, 1890), p. 85.

[99] *Liber de Delictis et Poenis Ecclesiasticis* (Romae, 1901), p. 311.

Wernz-Vidal,[101] Lega,[102] Pelle,[103] Ballerini-Palmieri,[104] Coronata,[105] Augustine,[106] and Beste[107] oppose Vermeersch.

Surely this list of authors is sufficiently long enough to demonstrate that the opinion demanding secrecy as an essential element in the phrase "*eiusdem generis*" is not as common as some claim.

A second argument employed by both Vermeersch and Ganzi to substantiate their opinion that a society must be secret to be similar to the Masons is the argument from history. It is their contention that since secrecy is constantly mentioned in the Pontifical documents condemning the Masons, it must be essential to the notion of "*eiusdem generis*."[108] However, upon close analysis of the documents cited by these authors it becomes evident that such a conclusion is not warranted.

There are four key papal constitutions on the subject of condemned societies. They are *In Eminenti* of Clement XII, dated April 28, 1738,[109] *Providas* of Benedict XIV, signed May 18, 1751,[110] *Ecclesiam* by Pius VII issued on September 13, 1821,[111] and finally the constitution of Leo XII which summarizes all the previous statements on the subject, *Quo Graviora* dated March 13, 1825.[112]

---

[100] *Il Diritto Penale Secundo il Codice di Diritto Canonico* (2 vols. in 1, Subiaco: Tipografia dei Monasteri, 1926-1930), II, 117.

[101] *Ius Canonicum ad Codice Normam Exactum* (7 vols. in 8, Romae: Universitas Gregoriana, 1923-1938), II, 482.

[102] *Praelectiones in Textum Iuris Canonici, De Delictis et Poenis* (2. ed., Romae, 1910), IV, 68.

[103] *Le Droit Pénal De L'Église* (Paris: P. Lethielleux, Libraire-Éditeur, 1939), p. 288.

[104] *Opus Theologicum Morale* (absolvit et editit D. Palmieri, 7 vols., Prati, 1889-1893), VII, 250.

[105] *Institutiones*, IV, 398-399.

[106] *A Commentary on Canon Law* (8 vols., St. Louis: B. Herder Book Co., 1931), VIII, 341.

[107] *Introductio in Codicem* (4. ed., Neapoli: D'Auria Pontificius Editor, 1956), p. 1037.

[108] Vermeersch, *op. cit.*, p. 63; Ganzi, *art. cit.*, pp. 106-114.

[109] *Fontes*, I, n. 299.

[110] *Fontes*, II, n. 412.

[111] *Fontes*, II, n. 479.

[112] *Fontes*, II, n. 481.

These constitutions comprise virtually all of the legislation of the Church on condemned societies. The later popes for the most part restated the same legislation. For example, the first document, *In Eminenti* of Clement XII provided that those who join or promote Masonic sects incur an excommunication reserved to the pope.[113] This censure was repeated by all the subsequent decrees and was substantially included in the constitution *Apostolicae Sedis.*[114] Eventually it was carried into the Code in canon 2335.

Moreover, the Roman Congregations, prior to the Code, issued a number of decrees dealing with problems that had arisen in applying to particular organizations the principles set forth in the papal statements on condemned societies. The authors who maintain that the history of legislation on condemned societies demonstrates that an organization must be secret in order to be similar (*eiusdem generis*) to the Masons, place great weight on these responses issued by the Roman Congregations. However, it will be shortly seen that no one of these decrees clearly states that secrecy is essentially required by the phrase *"eiusdem generis."*

Before examining these documents and decrees it is well to recall the historical background of the eighteenth and nineteenth centuries, the era in which this legislation was developed. During this period of time, secret societies, for a number of reasons, enjoyed an amazing expansion. In the United States, before the year 1880 there were 70 fraternal orders.[115] In the following decade 124 new secret societies were founded, while in the five years before 1895 there were 136 new societies. The United States possessed more secret societies and a larger number of "joiners" than all other nations, there being 6 million names on the rosters of fraternal societies by the end of the nineteenth century.[116]

Since the attraction to these groups operated no less for Catholics than others, these societies naturally presented the bishops of the United States with a complicated problem. Hence, many

---

[113] *Fontes,* I, n. 299.

[114] *Fontes,* III, n. 552, § II, n. 4, "Nomen dantes etc."

[115] MacDonald, *The Catholic Church and the Secret Societies in the United States* (ed. T. McMahon, New York, N. Y.: The United States Catholic Historical Society, Monograph Series XXII, 1946), p. 100.

[116] *Loc. cit.*

of the replies of the Congregations concerning condemned societies are in answer to appeals for solutions to problems proposed by the American bishops. Since these societies were springing up so rapidly, it was difficult for the American hierarchy to determine which should be condemned. Moreover, the types of organizations being formed in this country in some cases were entirely unlike the earlier European societies, and this also added to the difficulties in judging whether or not to condemn a particular group. It will be recalled that for a time even the early labor unions in the United States were under suspicion.

Therefore, it is only natural to find the papal statements and legislation from this period making frequent references to secret societies. It is important to remember this historical situation when considering the development of canon 2335 in pre-Code Law.

One of the documents cited by Ganzi[117] as proof that secrecy is required before a society can be classed as similar to the Masons is the constitution *Quo Graviora* by Leo XII, issued on March 13, 1825.[118] In this constitution Leo perpetually condemned all clandestine societies then existing, or which might exist. This means that joining these groups is prohibited *sub gravi.* The Pope then adds that those societies which set themselves against the Church or the state are prohibited perpetually under the same censure contained in the previous documents, namely, excommunication. The Latin text reads as follows:

> . . . societates occultas omnes tam quae nunc sunt, tam quae fortasse deinceps erumpent, et quae ea sibi adversus Ecclesiam et supremas civiles potestates proponunt quae superius commemoravimus, quocumque tandem nomine appellentur, Nos perpetuo prohibmemus sub eisdem poenis, quae continentur in praedecessorum Nostrorum literis in hac Nostra constitutione iam allatis, quas expresse confirmamus.[119]

---

[117] *Art. cit.*, p. 107.

[118] *Fontes*, II, n. 481.

[119] *Const. cit.*, pp. 729-730. The constitutions of his predecessors, mentioned by Pope Leo, are those of Clement XII, Benedict XIV, and Pius VII, cf. *supra*, p. 89.

Ganzi claims that the copula *et* most clearly indicates that the two elements of secrecy and machination provoked the condemnation.[120] However, the writer does not agree with this interpretation. It is true that secrecy causes the society to be condemned; that is, it is forbidden to join a society that is secret. But the reason why the society is condemned under censure is because it is machinating against the Church or the state. What Ganzi's interpretation does is make secrecy the formal motive for inflicting the censure, for if the society that is machinating against the Church or the state is not a secret society then it is not condemned under censure. Hence, it does not seem that this papal statement can be offered as proof that an organization must be secret in order to be similar to the Masons and hence subject to the censure of excommunication.

Ganzi also points to a number of decrees from the Roman Congregations as substantiating the opinion that secrecy is required.[121] For example, he cites the instruction sent to the bishops of Brazil in 1878. The pertinent section of this instruction reads:

> Praeterea Ordinarii, nomine S. Sedis, confessariis praecipiant, ut serio moneant suos poenitentes ne societati *franc maçons* aliisque huius generis clandestinis aggregationibus nomen dare, vel earum conventicula adire aut fovere praesumant, ac pertinacibus sacramentalem absolutionem negent. Ut autem vere resipiscentes absolvi queant ab excommunicatione incursa, Sanctitas sua necessarias et opportunas facultates Ordinariis concedit ad decennium.[122]

At this time Brazil was plagued by Masonic organizations as well as a number of other secret societies which were infiltrating into Catholic organizations for the laity and committing outrages against the Church.[123] This historical situation must be kept in mind when reading this document.

---

[120] "Ubi velim adnotes illa copula *et* clarissime ostendi duo elementa causam esse huius damnationis: quia occulta sunt et quia machinantur."—*Art. cit.*, p. 107.

[121] *Art. cit.*, pp. 107-110.

[122] *Fontes*, IV, n. 1056, 378.

[123] Cf. Quigley, *Condemned Societies*, pp. 89-93.

The Instruction says that penitents must be warned not to give their names to the Masons or other clandestine organizations of the same nature (*huius generis*). Now, what is the element that formally distinguishes the Masons and other clandestine organizations *"huius generis"?* It is the fact that the Masons are machinating against the Church or the state. In other words, the factor that places the Masons in a category or genus different from other societies is the fact that the Masons are machinating against the Church or the state. Secrecy is merely a mode of action, a means to an end, something accidental. Therefore, this Instruction actually substantiates the claim that it is the machination against the Church or the state which formally distinguishes the Masons from other societies, and hence is the reason why the Masons and other societies of the same *genus* are condemned under censure.

Another document discussed by Ganzi,[124] is the response of the Holy Office issued on August 5, 1846.[125] Quigley says that this reply was in answer to a question proposed by certain bishops of North America.[126] However, the document as it appears in the *Fontes* gives no indication as to the source of the question. The *dubium* proposed is this: *"Quaenam sint societates damnate in pontificiis constitutionibus?"* The Holy Office replies:

> Societates occultae, de quibus in pontificiis constitutionibus sermo est, eae omnes intelliguntur quae adversus Ecclesiam vel gubernium sibi aliquid proponunt, exigant vel non exigant a suis asseclis iuramentum de secreto servando.[127]

Admittedly, this is a most difficult response to interpret. Ganzi assumes, and quite freely, that what the questioner actually wanted to know was: Are all occult societies condemned under censure, or only some?[128] The Holy Office replied that only those that machinate against the Church or the state. From this response,

[124] *Art. cit.*, p. 108.
[125] *Fontes*, IV, n. 899.
[126] *Op. cit.*, p. 23.
[127] *Fontes*, IV, n. 899.
[128] *Art. cit.*, p. 108.

Ganzi concludes that two elements are therefore required before a society can be considered condemned under censure: it must be secret and it must be machinating against the Church or the state. However, even granting that Ganzi's assumption that the questioner really desired to know which *occult* societies are condemned under censure is a true assumption, the reply given by the Holy Office cannot be offered as proof that two elements are required: secrecy and machination. The reply of the Holy Office does not say that for a society to be condemned under censure it must be 1) occult, and 2) it must be machinating against the Church or the state. The reply merely says:

> Societates occultae, de quibus in pontificiis constitutionibus sermo est, eae omnes intelliguntur quae adversus Ecclesiam vel gubernium sibi aliquid proponunt, exigant vel non exigant a suis asseclis iuramentum de secreto servando.[129]

As Quigley notes the question asked, Which societies are condemned? was not answered.[130] What was said in the response is that occult societies spoken of in the pontifical constitutions were to be understood as all those which proposed to themselves anything against either the Church or the state.[131] What appears to be the true meaning of this response is offered by the editor of the *Acta Sanctae Sedis* in which this response also appears.[132] In commenting on the term *"occultae sectae,"* the editor of the *Acta Sanctae Sedis* says:

> Quare ex eo eiusmodi societates iam damnatae intelliguntur, quia *occultae sectae sunt,* id est societates spuriae, et adulterinae, quae ex praeposteris theoreticis principiis in subversionem publici ordinis, occultis subdolisque mediis, in sinu societatis organicam subsistentiam sibi comparant.[133]

[129] *Fontes,* IV, n. 899.
[130] *Op. cit.,* p. 58.
[131] *Loc. cit.*
[132] *ASS,* I, 290.
[133] *Ibid.,* p. 292.

The editor then gives a lengthy explanation of his statement. He points out that according to Divine Providence there are only two supreme, independent societies in the present order: the Church and the state, the latter being inferior and subordinated to the other by reason of its origin, means and end. Consequently, he says, any other society

> et potestas suprema et independens, quae neque civilis sit, neque ecclesiastica, utpote ordini praesenti divinae providentiae adversa, esse non potest nisi anomala et spuria.[134]

He then demonstrates that these occult or spurious societies attempt to make themselves supreme and independent by exercising, in their own name, judicial, legislative and coactive power over their members as well as over others. And finally, the editor of the *Acta Sanctae Sedis* rightly says that since there are only two supreme independent societies in the present order *"tertium illud societatem genus spurium dicendum est, earumdemque potestas, si ita appellari possit, erit tenebrarum potestas."*[135]

This commentary on the response of the Holy Office in question seems especially reasonable in the light of the second part of that response. Having said that occult societies are to be understood as those which propose to themselves anything against the Church or the state, the Holy Office then adds that the oath of secrecy is inconsequential.[136] And if the oath of secrecy is inconsequential, then secrecy itself is inconsequential. In other words, a society is not a secret society if it does not bind its members to secrecy. It should be remembered that the basic reason for forbidding Catholics to join secret societies is that the secrecy prevents the Church from inspecting the principles, teachings, methods and purposes of the organization, which is certainly the right and the duty of the Church. This is clearly brought out in the response given to Archbishop Kenrick in 1850. He asked the

---

[134] *Loc. cit.*

[135] *Ibid.*, p. 293.

[136] ". . . exigant vel non exigant a suis asseclis iuramentum de secreto servando."—*Resp. cit.*

Holy See whether those societies should be considered forbidden which, although they denied they machinated against the Church or the state, nevertheless bound themselves by oath or solemn engagement to secrecy.[137] The reply stated that these societies were comprehended in the Pontifical Constitutions.[138] Cardinal Fransconi, in a letter accompanying the response of the Holy Office, explained to the Archbishop the meaning of that short response, and how the secrecy and occultness with which these societies were enshrouded were the principal reasons for their condemnations. This was, the Cardinal added, to be the norm in the future.[139] Hence, the Third Plenary Council of Baltimore (1884) provided that if a doubt should arise concerning an individual society, whether or not it was forbidden, the rule to be followed in settling the doubt was the requirement of secrecy or of the oath or promise of blind and absolute obedience. Therefore, if a society so maintained its secrets as to be unwilling to reveal them to the competent authority of the Church, the society was to be regarded as forbidden.[140] Consequently, in case of doubt the ultimate criterion of whether or not membership should be forbidden in a society was whether or not it demanded an oath or promise of obedience or enjoined secrecy against inquiry by ecclesiastical authorities. But the response of 1846,[141] said that as far as occult societies are concerned, that is, those which propose to themselves anything against the Church or the state, it made no difference whether they demanded an oath of secrecy or not.

---

[137] *Concilii Plenarii Baltimorensis II, in Ecclesia Metropolitana Baltimorensi, a die VII, ad diem XXI Octobris, A. D. 1866 Habiti et a Sede Apostolica Recogniti Acta et Decreta* (Baltimorae: John Murphy, 1868), *appendix* XXVIII, pp. 335-336 (hereafter cited as *Concilii Plenarii Baltimorensis II*).

[138] "Comprehendi in Bullis Pontificiis."—*Ibid.*, p. 336.

[139] *Loc. cit.*

[140] "Si nempe ejusmodi societas aut ita secretum servandum injungat, ut neque auctoritati Ecclesiae illud manifestari sinat; aut si jusjurandum vel promissionem caecae absolutaeque obedientiae exigat, ea, praescindendo etiam a censuris, inter vetitas erit recensenda. . . ."—*Acta et Decreta Concilii Plenarii Baltimorensis Tertii, 1884* (Baltimorae: Typis Joannis Murphy et Sociorum, 1886), p. 138, n. 247.

[141] Cf. *supra*, p. 93.

The important element was the fact that the society was machinating against the Church or the state. This is brought out in a later instruction by the Holy Office. On May 10, 1884, the Holy Office issued a norm by which the two classes of societies could be distinguished, that is, those under censure and those merely prohibited. It reads:

> Ne quis vero errori locus fiat, cum diiudicandum erit, quaenam ex his perniciosis sectis censurae, quae vero prohibitioni tantum obnoxiae sint, certum imprimis est, excommunicatione latae sententiae multari massonicam aliasque eius generis sectas quae capite 2, n. 4 Pontificiae Constitutionis *Apostolicae Sedis* designantur, quaeque contra Ecclesiam vel legitimas potestates machinantur, sive id clam sive palam fecerint, sive exegerint sive non, a suis asseclis, secreti servandi iuramentum.[142]

Besides these, the Instruction goes on to say, there are also prohibited sects which are to be avoided under pain of grievous sin, among which are especially to be considered those that demand an oath of secrecy that may be revealed to no one, and absolute obedience to unknown leaders.[143]

In other words according to the clear wording of this Instruction, if a person joins a society that is openly machinating against the Church or the state, he incurs an excommunication. Moreover, this Instruction seems to make it perfectly clear that secrecy is of no importance in determining which societies are condemned under censure since it states that it matters not whether the society is operating openly or clandestinely. And yet, Vermeersch claims this Instruction does not weaken his position. He maintains that the words *palam seu clandestine* merely refer to the manner of acting.[144] Quigley answers Vermeersch's claim by noting that the specific charge against the Masons is that they *act* (*machinantur*) against the Church.[145]

---

[142] *Fontes,* IV, n. 1085, 417.

[143] "Praeter istas sunt et aliae sectae prohibitae atque sub gravis culpae reatu vitandae, inter quas praecipue recensendae illae omnes, quae a sectatoribus secretum nemini pandendum, et omnimodam obedientiam occultis ducibus praestandam iureiurando exigunt."—*Loc. cit.*

[144] *Op. cit.,* p. 67.

[145] *Op. cit.,* p. 59.

Quigley also answers Vermeersch's objection that the Instruction, although it states that an oath of secrecy is not required, it nevertheless hints of secrecy since it treats of denouncing occult leaders.[146] Quigley notes that the Instruction does not actually treat of denouncing occult leaders, and if it did, might it not easily mean that these occult leaders had to be denounced, if there were any such in the society? Moreover, taking the phrase, "*earumve occultos coriphaeos ac duces non denunciantes,* as found in the Constitution *Apostolicae Sedis,*[147] could not a society be non-secret and yet have some hidden leader or director?[148] A secret society implies more than occult leaders. It implies that the members are bound to reveal the secrets of the organization to no one.

Before closing this historical investigation into the development of canon 2335, it will be helpful to look briefly at the Third Plenary Council of Baltimore. This Council was held in the midst of these turbulent times and in one of the countries most plagued by these societies. The Council, in its section *De Societatibus Inhonestis,* cautions that the Masons and the Carbonari are not the only societies condemned under censure by the declarations of the Holy See. The condemnations and censures made by the Holy See must necessarily extend to all those societies of the same nature.[149] There is no mention here of secret or clandestine societies.

Again, in the pastoral letter issued by the Archbishops and Bishops assembled in the Council, in the section on forbidden societies, as a practical guide to the faithful, after stating that Catholics are forbidden to join groups which bind their members to secrecy or blind obedience, it then states:

> And if a society works or plots, either openly or in secret, against the Church, or against lawful authorities, then to be a member of it is to be excluded from the membership of the Catholic Church.[150]

[146] *Op. cit.,* p. 58.
[147] *Fontes,* III, n. 552, 27.
[148] Quigley, *op. cit.,* p. 59.
[149] *Acta et Decreta Concilii Plenarii Baltimorensis Tertii,* p. 138, n. 246.
[150] *Op. cit.,* p. xcvii.

These authoritative rules refer to societies that work against the Church or the state, and the rules make no reference to the notion of secrecy or clandestinity.

Finally, Archbishop Katzer, the noted Archbishop of St. Paul who was active in this Council, in an article on forbidden societies that appeared in 1892 says that the Third Plenary Council of Baltimore plainly enjoins that the Freemasons and Carbonari are excommunicated by name, and:

> that all other societies, though not mentioned by name, are excommunicated, if they are of the same nature as the Freemasons and Carbonari, that is, all those societies which openly or secretly plot (*machinantur*) against the Church, or against the lawful government, the state.[151]

So much for the historical development of the legislation on forbidden societies. Having examined the various papal statements and responses of the sacred congregations on this matter, it is apparent that no one of these documents clearly states that secrecy is essentially required by the phrase *"eiusdem generis."* It is true that there is frequent mention of secret societies in these statements, but this is only natural in view of the times and circumstances. Therefore, the historical development of the legislation on forbidden societies does not prove that *eiusdem generis* is not explained by the clause which follows in both the Constitution *Apostolicae Sedis*[152] and in canon 2335, *"quae contra Ecclesiam vel legitimas civiles potestates machinantur."*[153]

Cappello, in his 1950 edition of *De Censuris Iuxta Codicem Iuris Canonici,* is still of the opinion that the Communist Party should be considered under canon 2335.[154] He completely eliminates the

---

[151] Katzer, "Societies Forbidden in the Church," *The American Ecclesiastical Review* (*The American Ecclesiastical Review,* Vols. I-XXXIII, 1889-1905; from 1905: *The Ecclesiastical Review,* Philadelphia, 1905-1943; from 1944: *The American Ecclesiastical Review,* Washington, D. C.), VI (1892), 243.

[152] *Fontes,* III, n. 552.

[153] The Constitution *Apostolicae Sedis* has a slightly different wording, cf. *loc. cit.*

[154] *De Censuris Iuxta Codicem Iuris Canonici* (4. ed., Taurini-Romae: Marietti, 1950), p. 251 (hereafter cited as *De Censuris*).

arguments put forth by Ganzi by stating that he makes secrecy or clandestinity the formal reason for condemning the Masons and other such associations. Whereas, Cappello rightly says that secrecy or clandestinity is a secondary circumstance, a mere accidental.[155]

Moreover, it can be argued from the fact that surely the formulators of the Code of Canon Law were well aware of the two schools of thought on this question, and hence they would attempt to phrase the canon dealing with this subject in such a way as to eliminate the doubt. From a comparison of the wording of canon 2335 with the numerous pre-Code references to these societies, it seems evident that the formulators did clarify the difficulty. They entirely left out any mention of the words secret or clandestine. However, the word secret is used in canon 684, *"ab associationibus secretis."* It is also used in canon 1453 where it is stated that the *ius patronatus* cannot validly be transmitted to infidels . . . and those *"adscriptos societatibus secretis ab Ecclesia damnatis."* On the other hand, the phrase "Masons and other similar societies" is used several times in the Code and never in connection with secrecy.[156]

A final argument put forth by Ganzi is that *"eiusdem generis"* must refer to secrecy or clandestinity, otherwise the phrase is useless. If the phrase does not require secrecy, then the law should read, *"Nomen dantes sectae massonicae aliisve associationibus quae . . . machinantur. . . ."*[157] This argument is readily answered by pointing to the response of the Holy Office given to bishops of Brazil.[158] This response calls attention to the fact that the faithful are forbidden to give their names to Masonic sects *"aliisque huius generis clandestinis aggregationibus."* If *"genus"* refers to clandestinity, then the phrase *"huius generis"* is superfluous in this response given to the bishops of Brazil since the phrase is followed by *"clandestinis aggregationibus."*[159]

Moreover, the authors who hold for some form of secrecy or

---

[155] *Op. cit.*, p. 253, note 21.

[156] Canons 1240, § 1, 1°; 1399, 8°; 2335.

[157] *Art. cit.*, pp. 114-115.

[158] Cf. *supra*, p. 92.

[159] Cf. *supra*, p. 92.

clandestinity[160] set down no precise norms to determine what amount of secrecy is demanded. Must the laws and constitutions be secret? Must the leaders be occult? Hence, it is reasonable to presume that the legislator would not compose a law which, for all practical purposes, cannot be applied because of vagueness.

It should also be noted that canon 2335 is placed under the Title *De Delictis contra auctoritates, personas, res ecclesiasticas.* Obviously, the primary concern of the legislator here is the commission of crimes against authority or against the Church. It seems equally true that the legislator is not concerned with the type of organization attacking the Church or the state, secret or non-secret. Moreover, considering the *finis legis,* the protection of the Church and state, this cannot be accomplished by the legislator if the law is restricted only to those societies that are in some way secret.

It has been pointed out that some commentators on the Decree of the Holy Office issued in 1949 are of the opinion that this Decree confirms the opinion that the Communist Party does not fall under the provisions of canon 2335.[161] The commentators base this conclusion on the fact that when the Holy See was asked if it were lawful to join the Party it replied in the negative. The response further stated that those who knowingly and freely do join are to be refused the sacraments according to the ordinary principles governing the administration of the sacraments to those who are not properly disposed.[162] Hence, the conclusion reached by some is that merely joining the Party does not merit the excommunication provided in canon 2335, because the Holy Office does not consider the Communist Party a society similar to the Masons.

However, if the wording of questions 1 and 2 of the Decree

---

[160] Cf. e.g. Vermeersch, *op. cit.*, p. 64 sq.; Vermeersch-Creusen, *Epitome Iuris Canonici,* III, 330; Woywod, S., "Joining the Freemasons and Similar Societies," *Homiletic and Pastoral Review,* XXXVII (1937), 1282.

[161] Cf. *supra,* p. 85.

[162] *AAS,* XXXXI (1949), 334; *Digest,* III, 658-659.

of the Holy Office are carefully read it becomes evident that such a conclusion is not warranted.

Question n. 1 asks:

> Whether it is lawful to join the Communist Parties or favor them?

Question n. 2 asks:

> Whether it is licit to publish, propagate, or read books, periodicals, daily papers, or sheets which promote the doctrine or action of Communists, or to write in them.

The answer to both of these questions is in the negative. These two are followed by Question n. 3 which asks:

> Whether the faithful who knowingly and freely do the acts mentioned in 1 and 2 can be admitted to the sacraments.

The Holy Office replied:

> In the negative according to the ordinary principles governing the refusal of the sacraments to those who are not properly disposed.[163]

It is true that the response of the Holy Office does not say that those who join the Communist Party are excommunicated. However, it does not say that they are not excommunicated.[164] Nor can it be argued that the response implies that joining the Communist Party does not incur the excommunication of canon 2335, because the Holy See merely says that a person who performs such an act is to be refused the sacraments. It must not be for-

---

[163] *Loc. cit.*

[164] This point is mentioned by Bidagor, "Adnotationes," *Monitor Ecclesiaticus* (*Il Monitore Ecclesiastico,* Romae, 1876-1948; *Monitor Ecclesiasticus,* Romae, 1949-), LXXIV (1949), 53; cf. also Conway, "The Decree of the Holy Office on Communism," *The Irish Ecclesiastical Record,* LXXIII (1950), 61.

gotten that one of the effects of excommunication is that the person is forbidden to receive the sacraments.[165]

Moreover, it should be observed that the response to Question n. 3 refers not only to the act of joining the Communist Party, it also refers to all the acts mentioned in Question n. 2, which include publishing, propagating or reading books, periodicals, etc. In other words the response to Question n. 3 is a general answer, by way of common denominator, covering a number of acts which are forbidden by law. But it is to be noted that some of the acts mentioned in Question n. 2 are not only prohibited, but are also subject to the censure of excommunication. For example, canon 2318, § 1 inflicts an excommunication specially reserved to the Holy See on those who publish books of apostates, heretics or schismatics in which their doctrines are advocated.[166] Moreover, it is seen in the previous article[167] that a Catholic who professes Communism in the external forum is an apostate. Therefore, if such a person writes a book in which he advocates Communism, those who publish the book incur the excommunication provided in canon 2318. But in the reply to the question whether it is licit to publish, propagate or read books etc., which promote the doctrine of Communism, the Holy Office merely says that it is illicit and those who knowingly and freely perform said acts are to be refused the sacraments. It cannot be argued from this that therefore one who publishes the type of book just described is therefore not excommunicated, and should only be refused the sacraments. Similarly, it cannot be argued from the fact that the Holy Office says that those who join the Party are to be refused the sacraments that therefore they are not excommunicated.

When consideration is given to the very complex situation which the Holy See faced at the time of this Decree (1949), the wisdom and prudence of these answers become apparent. It is seen in the first chapter[168] that after the close of the Second World War the

[165] Canon 2260, § 1.

[166] Canon 2318, § 1: "In excommunicationem Sedi Apostolicae speciali modo reservatam ipso facto incurrunt, opere publici iuris facto, editores librorum apostatarum, haereticorum et schismaticorum, qui apostasiam, haeresim, schisma propugnant. . . ."

[167] Cf. *supra*, pp. 71-74.

[168] Cf. *supra*, pp. 55-60.

tactics of the Communists were so cleverly devised that the Party succeeded in convincing numerous Catholics that there was nothing incongruous in being a member of the Communist Party and a Catholic at the same time. More and more cooperation was being daily exhibited between the faithful and the Party, and in the 1948 elections in Italy the Communist Party and other left-wing groups massed some 8,000,000 votes. In many areas the Communist labor unions were in complete control, which meant that workers were obliged to belong to the Party in order to secure work. This was especially true in countries behind the Iron Curtain. The lamentable fact was that membership in the Party, even in areas outside the Iron Curtain was running into the hundreds of thousands, and many of these people were obviously Catholics. It was also apparent that many of these people did not realize that Catholics were forbidden to join the Party or render assistance to it. This fact is brought out in an anonymous commentary on the Decree of the Holy Office that appeared in *L'Osservatore Romano* a few weeks after the Decree appeared. It says in part:

> We can state next that in Western European countries the first part is more important than the second. In Italy, in Belgium, in France and so on there are many Catholics who, led astray by the promises of Communist leaders, or swayed by the desire for social reforms, favor Communism without accepting its fundamental doctrine. These, therefore, do not incur excommunication.[169]

In another section, the same commentary states the purpose of the Decree.

> The Decree seeks to open the eyes of those Catholics who allow themselves to be deceived by the false words of the propagandists of Communism.[170]

It might seem strange that a person could claim ignorance concerning the evils of Communism, especially when the Holy

---

[169] *L'Osservatore Ramano,* 27 July, 1949; translation from *The Tablet,* 194 (1949), n. 5698, 87.

[170] *Loc. cit.*

See has so frequently warned the faithful about this threat.[171] However, the situation was that *de facto* many were ignorant of the dangers of this movement, and the Holy See had to take this into account when she formulated this response. She had to reckon with the fact that many had joined the Party in good faith and hence in the internal forum would not have incurred the penalty provided in canon 2335. But once they realize that membership in the Communist Party is forbidden, they must sever their relationship with the Party, or they are to be refused the sacraments. The commentary just mentioned has this to say in commenting on the third response.

> The Third Reply is easily understood as well. It deals with the refusal of the sacraments to those who "knowingly" are guilty of the above-mentioned actions. Those who wish to remain members of a Communist movement, he who favors Communism, he who puts his own faith in jeopardy by reading the Communist Press, he who supports this Press, cannot ask to be admitted to the sacraments.[172]

It is worthy of note that the commentator makes no mention of the act of joining the Party. He refers only to those who "wish to remain members." Similarly, the commentator says that the people of Western Europe who, led astray by the promises of Communist leaders, favor Communism without accepting its fundamental doctrine do not incur excommunication. Here he is using the term "favor" in a general sense. He does not specifically mention the act of joining the Party.[173] This apparent intention to avoid treating the question of joining the Party is also seen in the closing section of the commentary in *L'Osservatore Romano*.

> Many Catholics support Communism by their votes at

[171] Cf. *supra*, pp. 41-58.

[172] *Art. cit., loc. cit.* It will be seen that the better opinion is that one who joins the Masons or a similar sect in good faith, and after learning that enrolling in said group is forbidden under censure, refuses to leave, does not incur the penalty, but cannot be admitted to the sacraments. Cf. *infra*, pp. 113-114.

[173] Cf. *supra*, p. 104.

> elections, with their money given to the Communist Press, with their support in social and political discussions, without wishing by this to adhere to the Communistic materialistic and anti-Christian doctrine. Therefore, they do not fall under the threat of excommunication.[174]

Again, there is no mention of joining the Communist Party.

In addition to the large numbers of the faithful who had unwittingly joined the Communist Party prior to 1949, the Holy See also realized that there must be others who freely joined, knowing that such an act was forbidden. The fact that the Decree of 1949 in question n. 3 employs the phrase *"scienter et libere"* does not preclude the possibility that a person could seriously violate the law and still be ignorant of the penalty.[175] This event is possible because the *scienter et libere* used in the Decree refers to the full advertence and full consent that is demanded in the commission of a mortal sin. In other words, it is the *scienter et libere* of moral theology. It is not the *scienter* or *libere* that is referred to in canon 2229, § 1, that is, perfect knowledge and full deliberation, or as it is frequently called, perfect *dolus*. The response cannot be demanding perfect *dolus* since, it will be recalled, this response also refers to the acts mentioned in Question n. 2. Now it has just been seen[176] that certain of the acts in Question n. 2 are subject to the censure provided in canon 2318, § 1, namely, publishing books of apostates which advocate apostasy. But this crime, as it is described in canon 2318, § 1, does not demand perfect *dolus*. Therefore, this response of the Holy Office would be demanding more than the Code. Consequently, the *scienter et libere* used in the response must refer to the knowledge and deliberation required before one can be accused of committing a serious sin. Hence, it is quite possible, indeed very probable, that a number of the faithful had knowingly and freely joined the Party prior to 1949, but were ignorant of the censure attached to that act. The Holy See had to face this problem, too.

---

[174] *Art. cit., loc. cit.*

[175] Question n. 3 reads: "Whether the faithful who knowingly and freely (*scienter et libere*) do the acts mentioned in 1 and 2 can be admitted to the sacraments." The reply was in the negative.

[176] Cf. *supra*, p.

The conclusion from this discussion is that it cannot be said that the response of the Holy Office favors the opinion that the Communist Party is not a sect similar to the Masons and therefore joining the Party does not incur the censure provided in canon 2335. In fact it seems that the very wording of the Decree favors the opinion that the Communist Party is a sect similar to the Masons. Why the Holy See chose not to treat the question directly is explained, at least in part, by the unusual circumstances which She faced at this juncture of history.[177] Undoubtedly, too, there were present other reasons known only to the Holy See. But the fact remains that both the historical development of the content of canon 2335 as well as the reading of the canon itself leave no doubt that the Communist Party must be considered as a society similar to the Masons.

Althought only a few manuals have been published since the appearance of this Decree of 1949, it is worth noting that Coronata's 1955 edition of *De Delictis et Poenis* lists the Communist Party under societies similar to the Masons.[178] Regatillo's 1951 edition of *Institutiones Iuris Canonici*, under the discussion on the privation of Christian burial, lists the Communist Party as a sect similar to the Masons.[179] Bouscaren-Ellis in their 1957 edition of *Canon Law, A Text and Commentary*, state that the "Communist Party certainly is" a society similar to the Masons.[180] Cappello, writing a year after the Decree of 1949, says that speculatively speaking those who join the Communist Party are subject to the censure of canon 2335. In practice, however, be-

[177] Conway, following the opinion that a sect must be clandestine to be similar to the Masons, states the reason why the excommunication of canon 2335 is not mentioned in the Decree is because if in a given country the Party is a secret society then the fact of joining it would involve the penalty of canon 2335.—*Art. cit.*, p. 61. Conway freely assumes this is the reason why canon 2335 is not mentioned. But it can just as readily be assumed that the Decree could have easily singled out clandestine parties as under censure. It can also be assumed that if clandestinity were required, the commentary in *L'Osservatore Romano* would have mentioned the fact.

[178] *Institutiones*, IV, 410.

[179] *Institutiones Iuris Canonici*, II, 65.

[180] *Canon Law, A Text and Commentary* (3. ed., rev., Milwaukee: The Bruce Publishing Co., 1957), p. 940.

cause of the *dubium,* he says, they are not bound.[181] The writer, however, fails to see any grounds for a real *dubium iuris.* It is true that some authors hold the opposite opinion. But this fact alone does not constitute a *dubium.* The authors must put forth sound arguments to demonstrate the validity of their opinion. To date, however, no author has advanced a convincing argument proving that the phrase *"eiusdem generis"* of canon 2335 requires secrecy. On the other hand, both the historical development of this canon, as well as the text of the law itself clearly indicate that a sect need not be clandestine or secret in order to qualify as an association similar to the Masons.

Therefore, one who joins the Communist Party incurs the penalty provided in canon 2335.

Section II. Requisites for Incurring the Penalty

Since the Communist Party is an association similar to the Masons (*eiusdem generis*), the conditions for incurring the penalty will be the same.

Nomen Dantes. This phrase should be interpreted as meaning the initial, overt act placed by the person, be it by writing, word, or deed, which act is recognized by the society as constituting membership. Moreover, the person must knowingly and freely join the organization.[182] Quigley says that it is sufficient that the person know that the sect he is about to join is condemned and that those who join it are excommunicated. He need not know, according to Quigley, that the society is actually machinating against the Church or the state.[183] However, it would be more correct to say that if the sect has been condemned *nominatim,* then there would be no need to know that the sect is striving to overthrow the Church or the state. But if the sect has not been condemned *nominatim,* then it is necessary to know that it is machinating. This is the only way the person can know that the sect falls under canon 2335, since this law inflicts the penalty

[181] *De Censuris,* p. 253.

[182] Cf. Ballerini-Palmieri, *Opus Theologicum Morale,* VII, 250; Cappello, *op. cit.,* p. 250; Coronata, *op. cit.,* 405; Quigley, *op. cit.,* p. 49.

[183] *Op. cit.,* p. 50.

on those joining the Masons and other sects militating against the Church or the state. Hence, some knowledge about the sect is necessary in order to know if it is similar to the Masons.[184]

Moreover, in order to incur the censure provided in canon 2335 the person must act freely. It was seen in the first chapter that in many countries behind the Iron Curtain membership in the Party is compulsory. It is also true that in many areas outside the Iron Curtain the Communist Party has gained control of such organizations as labor unions with the result that it is virtually impossible for people to secure work unless they belong to said unions. The commentary on the Decree of the Holy Office, appearing in *L'Osservatore Romano,* takes cognizance of this pressure.

> The Church, who must be watchful over the proper participation in the Sacraments, finds herself obliged to refuse them to those who prove unworthy. But she knows full well that there are some of the faithful who, against their own will, by moral and sometimes even physical force, are compelled to enroll themselves in a Communist Party. In such a case, the priest must be the judge of the circumstances under which the penitent has been compelled to accept the card of a party which he abhors and condemns in his heart.[185]

Therefore, generally speaking, it does not seem that joining the Communist Party is an intrinsically evil act, or one that involves a denial of the faith. If it were, then a person would be obliged to undergo death itself rather than give his name to the roster of a Communist Party.[186] But the use of the words *"scienter et libere"* in n. 3 of the Decree of 1949 of the Holy Office, as well as in the portion of the commentary in *L'Osservatore Romano* just quoted indicate that such is not demanded.

---

[184] Cappello demands that the person know the sect is machinating against the Church or state; *op. cit.,* p. 250.

[185] *L'Osservatore Romano,* 27, July, 1949; translation from *The Tablet,* 194 (1949), n. 5658, 87.

[186] Sirna, "Annotationes ad Decretum S. Officii de Communismo," *Apollinaris,* XXII (1949), 59-60.

Although canon 2335 appears under Title XIII of the Fifth Book of the Code, *De delictis contra auctoritates, personas, res ecclesiasticas,* it does not follow that the crime thereby necessarily involves the contempt of ecclesiastical authority mentioned in canon 2205, § 3. Such a contempt is present only in those delicts which involve a contemning of authority in a special manner, either because they are aimed directly against persons in authority or against their authority as such, or because they violate some command in such a way that the authority itself is necessarily and directly contemned.[187] An example of a crime involving this special contempt of ecclesiastical authority would be the crime of conspiracy against the authority of the Roman Pontiff or his legates, or against one's own Ordinary.[188] McCoy says that joining the Masons or some similar sect does not seem to involve this special contempt of authority.[189]

Therefore, because the act of joining the Communist Party *per se* is not an intrinsically evil act, nor does it generally amount to contempt of the faith, or a special contempt of ecclesiastical authority, then grave fear, even though relative, grave necessity and grave *incommodum* can be excusing causes.[190] It must be noted that the word *generally* is used here. In other words, there can be occasions and circumstances in which joining the Communist Party can amount to a contempt of the faith or a special contempt for ecclesiastical authority.[191] By way of example, a bishop, because of the activity and success of the Communist Party in his diocese, might undertake a campaign to warn his flock of the serious prohibition against joining the Communist

---

[187] Claeys Bouuaert, "De metus influxu quoad valorem actuum et quoad delicta et poenas secundum Codicem Iuris Canonici," *Jus Pontificium* (Romae: 1921), VI (1926), 139.

[188] Canon 2331, § 2.

[189] *Force and Fear in Relation to Delictual Imputability and Penal Responsibility,* pp. 95-96.

[190] Canons 2205, § 2, and 2229, § 3, 3°.

[191] "Adeo sollemnes et repetitae damnationes in sectam massonicam latae sunt, ut adhaesio, saltem *publica,* in contemptum auctoritatis ecclesiasticae necessario vergat (cfr. c. 2205, § 3). Quare ista adhaesio gravi incommodo vel metu excusari nequit."—Vermeersch-Creusen, *Epitome Iuris Canonici,* III, 331.

Party, or rendering assistance to it. If in the midst of the bishop's campaign, a prominent Catholic, for example, the mayor of the episcopal city, openly joins the Party, such an act could involve a special contempt of ecclesiastical authority. Grave fear, or grave *incommodum* can hardly be offered as an excusing cause in such circumstances.[192]

In the question of excusing causes, it should also be remembered that the causes alleged for excusing one from a censure will be acceptable in the external forum only if they can be demonstrated or proven in that forum.[193] The problem of administering the sacraments to a person who has not incurred the penalty in the internal forum, but who is obliged to observe the penalty in the external forum because of his external violation of the law, is treated in the final chapter.

Communist Parties. The Decree of the Holy Office states that it is forbidden to join (*nomen dare*) Communist Parties (*partibus communistarum*).[194] It is seen in the first chapter that the Communists make great use of organizations known as Fronts. They operate under names and for purposes which in no way suggest that these organizations or Fronts are subordinates of the Communist Party.[195] Although these groups seem to be seeking praiseworthy ends, e.g., World Peace Congress, nevertheless they are actually the advanced units of the Party, functioning under the strict supervision of Party officials, and for the purposes set by the Party.[196] Therefore, all these groups which are actually organized by and subject to the direction of the Communist Party must be included under the term Communist Parties. This con-

---

[192] Cf. canons 2229, § 3, 3°, and 2205, § 3.

[193] Canon 2200, § 2.

[194] Cf. *supra*, p. 59 for text. It should be noticed the *Digest*, III, 658, translates "*partibus communistarum*" as "Communist Party." More properly it should be "Communist Parties."

[195] Cf. *supra*, pp. 34-39.

[196] Pius XI wrote of these groups: "Under various names which do not even suggest Communism, they establish organizations and periodicals with the sole purpose of carrying their ideas into quarters otherwise inaccessible." —Pius XI, encycl. *Divini Redemptoris*—*AAS*, XXIX (1937), 95.

clusion is maintained in the commentary on the Decree of 1949 that appeared in *L'Osservatore Romano.*

> As the Communists may be divided into several parties (let us think of Yugoslavia) we speak of "parties" in the plural. To these must be added, next, the movements which are organized directly by Communism; for example, the Communist Youth Movement, the Communist Trade Unions properly-so called, and so on.[197]

Undoubtedly it will be objected by some that these groups do not fall under canon 2335 since frequently they are merely striving to realize some local need, oftentimes good in itself, and hence are not machinating against the Church or the state. A typical example of such an organization is the Communist trade union properly-so called.[198] But such an objection indicates an unfamiliarity with the techniques of the Communist movement. That these groups are actually part and parcel of the over-all Communist strategy is demonstrated in the first chapter and need not be repeated.

In discussing the requisites for incurring the penalty of canon 2335, it is seen that the person must know that the organization he is joining is machinating against the Church or the state.[199] This requisite is particularly applicable in the case of Communist Fronts. It is entirely possible in certain areas for people to be ignorant of the fact that a particular group is an affiliate of the Communist Party, especially in view of the fact that the Party is so clever in disguising its relationship with these groups. Therefore, a question arises concerning the canonico-juridical status of a person who joins the Party or one of these Fronts in good

---

[197] *Art. cit., loc. cit.*

[198] This term "Communist trade union properly-so called," used in the commentary just cited, refers to Fronts commonly found on the Continent. These are unions organized and openly operated by the Party. The Party's technique with regard to unions in the United States is described in the first chapter, cf. *supra,* pp. 37-38. These, too, under certain conditions, can fail under the term Communist union properly-so called, depending on the amount of control exercised by the Party.

[199] Cf. *supra,* pp. 108-109.

faith. Generally speaking, the person is bound to observe the penalty in the external forum until he is able to prove his ignorance in that forum.[200] Naturally, too, severance from the group is required. However, if the person joins in good faith and subsequently learns that joining said group is forbidden under censure, but refuses to separate from the organization, does he then incur the penalty? The authors do not agree on this point. D'Annibale says that such a person escapes the penalty only if he remains in the organization unwillingly. He offers no reasons for this statement, however.[201] Lehmkuhl is of the opinion that the penalty would not be incurred if the person refused to separate immediately from the group after learning that joining the organization was forbidden under censure. However, he would incur the penalty when thereafter he placed the first act that proved him a member of the sect.[202] Noldin, in his pre-Code edition of his work *De Poenis Ecclesiasticis,* holds the same opinion as D'Annibale.[203] Cappello says the person certainly contracts the penalty if he does not have a proportionate reason for not leaving the organization, for example, grave harm will come to him if he resigns.[204] Quigley, following Chelodi,[205] holds what appears to be the better opinion, namely, that the canonical offense punished in the law is the act of joining the group.[206] Therefore, one who joins the Communist Party in good faith, but subsequently learns that his act is forbidden under censure, does not incur the penalty of canon 2335 if he refuses to separate from the Party. The reason for this opinion is that the term *"nomen dantes"* must be interpreted strictly.[207] Quigley points out that *nomen dans* refers only to the one enlisting, enrolling or joining. Hence, one having enlisted, or joined

---

[200] Canon 2200, § 2; exceptions to this principle are treated in the final chapter.

[201] *Summa Theologica Moralis,* I, 391.

[202] *Theologica Moralis,* II, 703.

[203] *De Poenis Ecclesiasticis* (5. ed., Oeniponte, 1905), p. 67.

[204] *Op. cit.,* p. 250.

[205] *Ius Poenale et Ordo Procedendi in Iudiciis Criminalibus* (Tridenti: Libr. Edit. Tridentum, 1925), p. 90.

[206] *Op. cit.,* pp. 52-55.

[207] Canon 2219, § 1.

would no longer be a *nomen dans,* but a *nomen dedit.*[208] In other words, the precise crime punished by canon 2335 is the initial overt act placed by the person, be it by writing, word, or deed, which act is recognized by the organization as constituting membership. The authors who hold the opposite opinion not only confuse the internal and external forum, they also seem to impose the penalty on the person for not leaving the sect. But it must be kept in mind that the law is directed toward the prohibition of joining sects which machinate against the Church or the state. It is on account of the joining of the sect, and on that account alone, that the penalty is incurred.[209]

Since, then, *nomen dans* cannot be applied to one who has already joined the sect condemned under censure, and since it is forbidden to extend a penalty from one case to another, it remains that one who joins the Party in good faith, and later on, when that good faith is destroyed, does not withdraw, would not come under the penalty of canon 2335. However, in the external forum the person will be presumed subject to the penalty.[210]

In closing, it should be said that whether or not the delinquent takes an active part in the Party, or perhaps never attends a meeting has no bearing on the question. The crime punished in canon 2335 is the act of joining (*nomen dantes*) the Masons or a sect of the same nature.

Section III. Is the Communist Party an Atheistic Sect?

In 1934 the Pontifical Commission for the Authentic Interpretation of the Code of Canon Law issued a response in answer to the following question:

> Whether according to the Code of Canon Law persons who belong or have belonged to an atheistic sect are to be considered as regards all legal effects, even those

[208] *Op. cit.,* p. 54.

[209] It is true that canon 1240, § 1, 1° employs the word adherents (*addicti*) and not the term *nomen dantes,* but it is not permitted to extend a penalty from one case to another even if the reason is alike in both or more compelling in the latter; cf. canon 2219, § 3.

[210] Canon 2200, § 2.

> which concern sacred ordination and marriage, the same as persons who belong or have belonged to a non-Catholic sect.

The reply was in the affirmative.[211]

Now, if the Communist Party is an atheistic sect within the sense of this response, then it necessarily follows that a person who joins the Communist Party, or who had once joined it in the past, is considered as regards all legal effects, even those which concern sacred ordination and marriage, the same as a person who belongs, or has belonged to a non-Catholic sect.[212] Moreover, if the Communist Party is the type of atheistic sect envisioned in the response of 1934, then merely joining the Party is an act that verges on contempt of faith, and therefore the person cannot offer grave fear, necessity or *incommodum* as excusing causes.[213] Under certain circumstances, too, joining the Communist Party, if it is an atheistic sect, will create a violent suspicion that the person has abandoned the faith and hence will be subject to the provisions of canon 2314, § 1.[214] And finally, a person who professes Communism and joins the Party or publicly adheres to it if it is an atheistic sect, brands himself as infamous (*infamia iuris*) because of his association with an atheistic sect.[215]

These conclusions, of course, are based on the assumption that the Communist Party, as such, is the type of atheistic sect envisioned in the response of 1934. The purpose of this section is to show that such a general assumption is not true. In other words, the purpose of this section is to demonstrate that the Communist Party can be considered as an atheistic sect, according to the sense of this response, only under certain conditions.

Certainly it cannot be argued that the philosophy of Communism is not atheistic. That should be obvious.[216] However, because the

---

[211] *AAS,* XXVI (1934), 494; *Digest,* II, 286-287.

[212] Some of the canonico-juridical effects that follow from the act of joining an atheistic sect are considered in the final chapter; cf. *infra,* pp. 152-154, 159.

[213] Cf. canon 2228, § 3, 3°.

[214] Cf. *supra,* pp. 78-80 concerning suspicion.

[215] Canon 2314, § 1, 3°.

[216] *Cf.* Pius XI, encycl. *Divini Redemptoris,* 31 March, 1937—*AAS,* XXIX (1937), 65-106; this is Pius XIth's encyclical on atheistic Communism; cf. also *supra,* pp. 47-55.

philosophy of Communism is atheistic, it does not follow that the Communist Party is therefore the type of atheistic sect envisioned by this response of 1934. In order to demonstrate this proposition, two points must be considered: the precise meaning of the term atheistic sect used in the response; and secondly, the exact position or role of atheism in the philosophy of Communism must be determined. But prior to investigating these two considerations, it should be kept in mind that since there is question here of inflicting a penalty and restricting a person's rights, a strict interpretation is demanded as to law and as to fact.[217]

Maroto, in an excellent commentary on this response of 1934, clearly sets forth the precise meaning of the term atheistic sect and what is required before an organization can qualify as such a sect.[218] According to Maroto, a society, even though one of its chief tenets is the denial of God, cannot be considered a true and *proprie dicta* atheistic sect according to the sense of this response unless the organization professes atheism as its particular, primary and proper end. Moreover, atheism must be the principal source and foundation of the organization's doctrinal system, the fountainhead of its other doctrinal errors, norms of living and acting.[219] Therefore, he concludes, an atheistic sect, according to the norm of this response, can only be understood as one which is a true assembly (*coetus vel congregatio*) of men, professing theoretical

---

[217] Canon 19, canon 2219, § 1.

[218] "Annotationes Super Responsis Die 30 Iulii 1934 Datis a Pontif. Commissione Ad Codicis Canones Authentice Interpretandos," *Commentarium pro Religiosis* (from 1935: *Commentarium pro Religiosis et Missionariis*, Romae: 1920-), XV (1935), 337-346; cf. also Poglajen, "Les Différentes Organisations Athées," *Nouvelle Revue Théologique* (Paris, 1869—), LXI (1934), 1069-1073; Jombart, "Annotations," *Nouvelle Revue Théologique*, LXI (1934), 1077-1078.

[219] "Tandem societates etiam, quae inter sua capita doctrinalia ferant pariter Dei negationem et colant atheismum, non sunt habendae tamquam *verae* et *proprie dictae sectae aetheisticae* ad sensum responsi nunc a Pontificia Commissione lati, si ipsum atheismum minime habeant tamquam peculiarem, primarium et proprium suum finem, et veluti caput praecipuum et fundamentum sui systematis doctrinalis, unde sicut e fonte promanent ad instar rivulorum ceteri errores, normae vivendi, et agendi etc."—*Art. cit.*, pp. 338-339.

and practical atheism as its proper religious doctrine, or more correctly, irreligious doctrine, and maintaining atheism as its proper doctrinal system, and its primary special end.[220]

It remains now to consider the position of atheism in the philosophy of Communism in order to determine whether or not atheism is the particular, primary and proper formal end of Communism.

It is stated in the introduction to the first chapter that some knowledge of the theory and practice of Communism is necessary before a true judgment could be made concerning the canonico-juridical status of a person who associates himself with this movement. In the particular question under discussion here, such knowledge is surely required. Upon examining the history of the development of Communist philosophy, it is seen that the theorists, Marx and Engels, did not begin with the false principles of atheism and then construct their system around the denial of God. Rather, their point of departure was materialism, which naturally implied a denial of God. Starting with materialism, Marx "turned Hegel's dialectic upside down and made it the basis of a complete philosophical system of dialectical materialism."[221] He applied the dialectic to nature, the mind, history, the state, society, and so on. Naturally enough, he also applied it to religion. Both Marx and Engels readily adapted the then current Darwinian theory of evolution and applied it to religion.[222] This application did away

---

[220] "*Secta* ergo *atheistica*, ad normam huius responsi, de quo agimus, ea solummodo intelligenda est quae sit verus coetus vel congregatio hominum profitentium theorice et practice atheismum stricte dictum tamquam peculiarem doctrinam religiosam (dicas potius irreligiosam), illumque teneant veluti proprium systema doctrinale et ceu primarium finem praecipue et directe intentum."—*Loc. cit.;* Ganzi says that an atheistic sect must be, in a sense, a *secta religiosa*, that is "quae directe et immediate, ex interna sua constitutione et organizatione, pro fine habeat, saltem principaliori modo activitatem religiosam, sive pro, sive contra; in case nostro, apostasiam seu atheismum promovere."—*Art. cit.*, p. 105; Coronata, *op. cit.*, p. 301; cf. also Ottaviani's treatment of the nature of a society "ex fine determinantur," in his *Institutiones Iuris Publici Ecclesiastici* (3. ed., 2 vols., Romae: Typis Polyglottis Vaticanis, 1947-1948), I, 42.

[221] McFadden, *The Philosophy of Communism*, p. 34.

[222] *Ibid.*, p. 275.

with the supernatural origin of religion and fitted nicely into their dialectical system. The conclusion they reached was that religion had its origin among primitive people and passed through many stages of development and evolution. The chief purpose of religion, according to Marx and Engels, is to soothe the irritation which naturally exists between opposing classes. It teaches the poor the blessings of poverty, and encourages the rich to give alms. However, religion thereby justifies and renders permanent the present economic arrangement which necessarily brings with it the exploitation of the masses.[223] In a word, religion is the opium of the people, says the Communist philosophy.

As for the future of religion, the Communist theory asserts that since religion is somewhat of a reflex arising from the exploitation of the masses, it will naturally continue to exist in society as long as such exploitation lasts.[224] In short, as long as man is the victim of oppression he will need the opium of religion to furnish him an "escape" from reality.[225] As McFadden remarks, one can readily perceive that "religion does not rank as a basic problem for Communism."[226] This is plainly evident from the following quotation from Lenin:

> The unity of that genuinely revolutionary struggle of the oppressed class to set up a heaven on earth is more important to us than a unity in proletarian opinion about the imaginary paradise in the sky. That is why we do not declare, and must not declare in our programme that we are atheists; that is why we do not forbid and must not forbid proletarians who still cling to the remnants of old prejudices to come into closer contact with our Party. . . . We must not allow the forces waging a genuinely revolutionary economic and political struggle to be broken up for the sake of opinions and dreams that are of third-rate importance, which are rapidly losing all political significance, and which are being steadily relegated to the rubbish heap by the normal course of economic development.[227]

---

[223] *Ibid.*, p. 125.
[224] *Ibid.*, p. 127.
[225] *Loc. cit.*
[226] *Op. cit.*, p. 128.
[227] *Religion* (New York: International Publishers, 1933), p. 10.

Since Communist philosophy does not consider religion a major problem, then its attack on religion appears to be inconsistent with its principles. McFadden solves this by pointing out that the Communist attack on religion is not an inconsistency in the system. Organized religion, according to Communist plans, must be abolished if the ruling class is to be overthrown.[228] One may observe, moreover, that for this reason the Church is being attacked today in countries behind the Iron Curtain. The movement realizes that it must overcome organized religion if it is to annihilate the present civilization. But it also is of the opinion that there will be economic suffering in society until true Communism arrives and relieves man of his need for religion. "For that reason," says McFadden, "it tolerates private religious belief and religious sentiment in the transitional stage of the Dictatorship of the Proletariat."[229]

Since the time of the Second World War, the Communist Parties in a number of countries in no way demand an avowal of atheism. For example, the Constitution of the Communist Party of the United States, adopted in 1945, stated that any resident of the United States, regardless of race, color, national origin, or religious belief, was eligible for membership.[230] Moreover in many countries members of the Party still maintain their affiliations with churches.

From what has been stated it should be evident that atheism is not the primary, particular, and proper end of Communism. Nor is it the source and foundation of the organization's doctrinal system, the fountainhead of its other doctrinal errors. As McFadden writes:

> . . . any criticism of Communism which is directed primarily against its atheistic character is not, of itself, a sufficient criticism of the theory. The criticism of its philosophy of history is much more fundamental and necessary.[231]

---

[228] *Op. cit.*, p. 130.

[229] *Op. cit.*, p. 131.

[230] For full text, cf. *supra*, p. 30.

[231] *Op. cit.*, p. 129.

Moreover, as Ganzi notes, an organization that does not demand adherence to atheism, and permits its members to practice their religion cannot be termed an atheistic sect in the sense of the response of 1934.[232] That the Party is not such a sect as envisioned by this response can also be seen when one considers sects that are patently atheistic in the sense of the response. For example, in 1929 the Federation of Militant Atheists was organized in Russia. It launched a systematic attack against all religion and used every possible means to cultivate and spread atheism. However, it is important to note that not all the members of the Communist Party in Russia at that time were members of the Federation, and *vice versa.*[233] Maroto says that without a doubt authorities at the Holy See had this and other similar organizations in mind when they issued this response in 1934.[234] At that time there were numerous other atheistic sects operating in various countries, oftentimes in close cooperation. In Belgium there was the Materialist League; in Japan, The Militant League Against Religion; in Poland, The Federation of Polish Free Thinkers, and so on.[235] All of them had atheism as their primary, proper, and particular end.

In conclusion, therefore, the Communist Party, *qua talis,* should not be classified as an atheistic sect in the sense of the response of 1934. However, two observations must be made. First, it should be evident that this whole discussion on the atheistic phase of Communism is concerned only with the canonical problem of determining whether or not the Party should be classified as an atheistic sect. In no way is it intended to minimize the atheistic factor in this movement. But, as was stated in the beginning of this section, since a penalty is involved in the question, the law demands that a strict interpretation be given.

Secondly, although the Communist Party, *qua talis,* should not be considered as an atheistic sect, if *de facto* in some area the

---

[232] *Art. cit.,* p. 105.

[233] Poglajen, *art. cit.,* p. 1070.

[234] *Art. cit.,* p. 339. He specifically excludes the Communist sects, even though they profess atheism among their other doctrinal errors.—*Loc. cit.*

[235] Poglajen, *art. cit.,* p. 1070.

Party is actually professing atheism as its primary, proper and particular end, then the Party there must be considered as an atheistic sect within the response of 1934. Ottaviani notes this in his commentary on the decree of the Holy Office concerning marriages of Communists.[236] In such a case the provision of canon 2314, § 1, 3° is applicable. Hence, if one who has externally professed Communism will have joined (*nomen dederint*) a Communist Party of this kind, or publicly adhered to same, the person renders himself infamous. Publicly adhering to a sect of this kind should not be restricted to the notion of formal membership. True, the term adhering to a sect can include membership, but it is broader than membership. One who publicly defends the teaching of such a sect, or frequents its meetings can be said to adhere to it without actually being a formal member. That is without having performed some act which is accepted by the organization as constituting membership.

Moreover, a person who joins the type of Communist Party envisioned by the response of 1934 must be considered as regards all legal effects, even those which concern sacred ordination and marriage, the same as one who belongs or has belonged to a non-Catholic sect. Since the act of joining such a Party is in contempt of the faith, grave fear, necessity or incommodum cannot be offered as excusing causes.[237]

ARTICLE 3. THOSE WHO FAVOR THE COMMUNIST MOVEMENT

Introduction

The purpose of the present article is to determine the canonico-juridical status of those who show favor to the Communist movement. The article is divided into three sections. The first section examines the meaning and scope of the term "favoring the Communist movement." The second and third sections deal with a

[236] "Profecto sub hac acceptione verborum, sectae atheisticae veniunt solummodo *communistae illi* qui nonnullis in regionibus speciales consociationes constituunt quarum proprius et speciales finis est negare Deum, omnemque religionem. Hae sectiones sunt et dici debent *sectae atheisticae*."—"De Communistarum Matrimoniis," *Apollinaris,* XXII (1949), 103.

[237] Canons 2205, § 3; 2229, § 3, 3°.

number of specific acts which are frequently performed in behalf of the Communists, for example, publishing and selling Communist literature, turning children over to associations formed by the Communists for the education of youth. Although several of the acts treated in the latter two sections actually pertain to the crime of professing Communism, the writer has included them in the present article because they are closely related to the subject matter at hand, namely, favoring the Communist movement.

Section I. The Meaning and Scope of the Term "Favoring the Communist Movement"

The first question of the Decree of the Holy Office issued in 1949 asked "Whether it is licit to join the Communist Parties or to favor them." The reply stated:

> In the negative: for Communism is materialistic and anti-Christian; and the leaders of the Communists, even though they sometimes verbally profess that they are not attacking religion in fact nevertheless by doctrine and action show themselves to be enemies of God and of the true religion and the Church of Christ.[238]

This Decree makes it clear that it is illicit to show favor to the Communist Parties, which are the vehicles for the propagation of Communist philosophy and purposes. That it is morally wrong to aid this movement had already been stressed by Pius XI in his famous encyclical on Communism. Addressing the bishops of the world, he said:

> Venerable Brethren, take the greatest precaution that the faithful avoid these snares. Since Communism is intrinsically evil whoever wants to save Christianity and civilization from destruction must refrain from aiding it in the prosecution of any project whatever.[239]

---

[238] *AAS,* XXXXI (1949), 334; *Digest,* III, 658-659. The writer has modified the translation found in the *Digest* to read "Communist Parties." This is more in conformity with the Latin text, *"partibus communistarum."*

[239] Pius XI, encycl. *Divini Redemptoris,* 31 March, 1937—*AAS,* XXIX (1937), 96.

In the Pre-Code Law of the Constitution *Apostolicae Sedis,* those who favored the Masons and other similar sects incurred the same penalty as those who joined these groups. The Constitution stated that an excommunication specially reserved to the Holy See was incurred by:

> Nomen dantes sectae *Massonicae* aut *Carbonariae* aut aliis eiusdem generis sectis quae contra Ecclesiam vel legitimas potestates seu palam, seu clandestine, machinantur, necnon iisdem sectis favorem qualemcumque praestantes. . . .[240]

The present law of the Code dealing with the crime of joining the Masons and other similar sects does not mention the crime of favoring these groups. Canon 2335 simply states:

> Nomen dantes sectae massonicae aliisve eiusdem generis associationibus quae contra Ecclesiam vel legitimas civiles potestates machinantur, contrahunt ipso facto excommunicationem Sedi Apostolicae simpliciter reservatam.

Since the present law makes no mention of the crime of favoring the Masons and other similar sects, Vermeersch-Creusen,[241] Aryinhac,[242] and Quigley[243] rightly state that the Code has suppressed the excommunication against those who favor the Masons and other similar sects.[244] As Quigley notes, it does not seem possible that the members of the Commission for Codification did not have the regulations of the Constitution *Apostolicae Sedis* before their eyes and minds when framing canon 2335.[245] Moreover, canon 19 directs that laws establishing penalties must be interpreted strictly, and canon 2219, § 3 says that penalties cannot be extended from one case to another, even though there is no equal or even greater reason. Hence, since the Code omits the term

[240] *Fontes,* III, n. 552, § II, n. 4.
[241] *Epitome Iuris Canonici,* III, 277.
[242] *Penal Legislation in the New Code of Canon Law,* p. 241.
[243] *Condemned Societies,* p. 50.
[244] Cf. also canon 6, 5°.
[245] *Op. cit.,* p. 50.

favor in canon 2335, favoring these organizations is no longer punished under this canon. However, those who knowingly and freely favor the Communist Party or the Communist movement are to be refused the sacraments.[246] For that reason, it will be helpful to have some understanding of what this term favor implies.[247]

The term *favor* or *fautor* has a long history in canonical legislation. For centuries, the famous *Bulla Conae Domini*[247] contained an excommunication for all those who *favored* apostates, heretics, or schismatics.[248] *Fautores* were also punished by the penalty of excommunication under the Law of the Constitution *Apostolicae Sedis*.[249] The term was also used, as has already been noted,[250] in the Constitution *Apostolicae Sedis* in the section dealing with the Masons and other similar sects.[251]

The authors who commented on these *Bullae Coenae Domini* usually provided an explanation of the term *favor* or *fautor*. Sanchez's explanation is typical.[252] He divides *fautores* into two groups: those who offended positively, and those who offended

---

[246] This is clearly stated in the Decree of 1949; cf. *supra*, pp. 59-60. Poverty of matter naturally enters into the question, but this is more properly in the realm of moral theology.

[247] The *Bulla Coenae Domini*, issued annually by the Popes on Holy Thursday contained, among other items, a list of crimes and their punishments. This practice goes back to at least the 15th century. Cf. Alterius, *Disputationes de Censuris Ecclesiasticis* (Romae: 1616), I, Lib. V, cap. 3, disp. 1, p. 448.

[248] A typical example is found in the *Bulla Coenae Domini* of Paul V, 8 April, 1610: "Excommunicamus et anathematizamus . . . a Christiana fide apostatas ac omnes et singulos alios haereticos quocumque nomine censeantur . . . ac eis credentes, eorumque receptatores, fautores, et generaliter quoslibet illorum defensores."—*Magnum Bullarum Romanum* (19 vols. in 18, Luxemburgi, 1727-1754), II, 282.

[249] "Omnes a christiana fide apostatas et omnes ac singulos haereticos, quocumque nomine censeantur . . . eisque credentes, eorumque receptores, fautores, ac generaliter quoslibet illorum defensores."—*Fontes*, III, n. 552, § I, n. 1.

[250] Cf. *supra*, p. 123.

[251] *Fontes*, Vol. III, n. 552.

[252] *Operis Moralis in Praecepta Decalogi* (2 vols., Parmae, 1723), I, Lib. II, cap. X, pp. 114-115.

negatively. He also employed the terms "sins of commission" and "sins of omission." Acts of omission were principally committed by those who possessed positions of authority, such as magistrates or bishops. Sanchez also presents a list of acts which would be considered favoring apostates—sins of commission. For example, a person would be favoring an apostate if he offered excuses for the apostates, praised or commended his activities. Moreover, giving advice to apostates, assisting them to escape the law, falsifying testimony concerning them were also listed as acts that showed favor to apostates.[253]

Piatus, commenting on the Constitutione *Apostolicae Sedis,* said the term *fautores* included all who gave assistance to heretics in order that their errors might more easily be diffused.[254] For example, he said that those whose words or actions assisted the circulation of the errors of apostates must be classified as positively cooperating with the crime. Noldin, in his pre-Code work, described negative *fautores* as those who were bound by reason of some office to impede the advancement of heresy and failed to act. Positive *fautores* were those who by their words praised or commended heretics, or by their deeds, for example, offering money, assisted in the spreading of errors.[255]

Wernz held that those who favored a delinquent after the commission of his crime, for example, by defending him, normally should not be classified as cooperators or accomplices. To be a cooperator or an accomplice, he correctly notes, one must have some influence on the commission of the crime.[256] However, Wernz remarks that for the more serious crimes, the Church frequently punishes those who favor the criminal. He cites the example of those who favor apostates.[257] Later, in his discussion on apostasy, Wernz presents the twofold division of *fautores,* that is, those who

---

[253] *Loc. cit.*

[254] *Commentarium in Constitutionem Apostolicae Sedis* (Tornaci, 1881), p. 11.

[255] *De Poenis Ecclesiasticis,* p. 43.

[256] *Ius Decretalium* (6 vols., Vols. I-IV, 2. ed., 1905-1912; Vols. V-VI, 1913-1914, Romae: Prati), VI, 63.

[257] *Loc. cit.* Under the Constitution *Apostolicae Sedis* those who favored apostates were excommunicated; cf. *supra,* p. 123.

assist in the spreading of heretical doctrines either by sins of omission or sins of commission.[258]

Coronata, to cite one of the post-Code authors who treat the term *fautor,* presents the traditional explanation of the word.[259] A person can favor heresy either positively or negatively. A person who is bound *ex officio* to prevent the spread of heresy, if he fails to act, assists the propagation of hertical doctrines in a negative way. Those who praise heretics *qua tales,* those who excuse them, commend them, or instruct heretics in the best methods to use in spreading their errors or avoiding condemnation are to be considered as favoring heresy in a positive fashion. He also includes under this notion the contribution of money. Augustine lists under the term *fautores* those who write for heretics, praise their methods and objects or recommend their works and give them material support.[260]

This traditional meaning assigned to the term *favor* by the authors can be of some service in understanding the term as it is used in the Decree of 1949 of the Holy Office. Hence, favoring the Communist Party or Communism will include two aspects. It will include those who negatively assist, that is, those in official positions who are obliged in virtue of their office to hinder the spread of Communism. It will also include those who favor the Party or the movement in a positive way by assisting in the propagation of the errors of Communism. Therefore, it is forbidden to attend Communist meetings, foster programs of the Party, attend their social events ("festivals"), promote their cultural or political programs, contribute funds, vote for them, subscribe to their newspapers or periodicals, or run advertisements in them.[261] It must always be kept in mind that meetings, social functions, political programs, literature, etc., are part and parcel of the Communist strategy and tactics, and cannot be isolated from the movement, regardless of how innocent they might appear.

---

[258] *Op. cit.*, p. 294.

[259] *Institutiones,* IV, 310.

[260] *A Commentary on Canon Law,* VIII, 288.

[261] Sirna, "Annotationes ad Decretum S. Officii de Communismo," *Apollinaris,* XXII (1949), 64. Communist literature is treated more fully in the next section.

Therefore, anyone who persists in favoring the Communist movement must generally be refused the sacraments since he is not properly disposed.[262] But this also should be noted. If a person performs certain acts in favor of the Communist movement, and these acts create a vehement suspicion concerning the state of his mind, then he is suspect of heresy.[263] In that event the person must be warned by the proper authority to remove the causes of suspicion. If the warning proves fruitless, the suspected person must be forbidden to perform ecclesiastical legal acts, according to canon 2265. If he is a cleric, he must be suspended *a divinis,* after a second warning has been left unheeded. If within six months thereafter he has not removed the suspicion, he must be regarded as a heretic and subject to the penalties of canon 2314.[264]

Moreover, if a person's neglect of his religious duties and the acts he performs in favor of Communism are such that they create a violent suspicion that he is actually professing Communism, then he will fall under the provisions of canon 2314. As has been seen earlier,[265] because of the nature of circumstantial evidence upon which suspicion is based, no hard and fast rule can be set down to distinguish the various degrees of suspicion—violent, vehement, and light. Each case must be examined and judged in the light of the circumstances of time and place, keeping in mind that violent suspicion is equivalent to moral certitude.

Finally, the canon on cooperation has application here in this discussion on favoring Communism.[266] For example, a person, in abuse of some authority, domestic or otherwise, might command others to join the Communist Party. Such a person can rightly be called a *mandans.*[267] One might also induce others to join the Party by promising money or other temporal advantages, or by threatening them with some loss, or danger. Again, a person might

---

[262] When material cooperation can be tolerated must be determined according to the rules of moral theology.

[263] Canon 2316; cf. *supra,* pp. 78-80; cf. also Vermeersch-Creusen, *Epitome Iuris Canonici,* III, 317.

[264] Canon 2315.

[265] Cf. *supra,* pp. 79-80.

[266] Canon 2209.

[267] Canon 2209, § 3.

communicate with the Communist Party, thus enabling another person to join. All these cases, except the *mandans,* are based on the assumption that the Party would not have been joined without their cooperation. Hence, granted that persons cooperated in these ways in getting a new member and the new member would not have become a member of the Communist Party without their cooperation, then canon 2209, § 3 would bind them under canon 2335. The same principles of cooperation can be applied to canon 2314, the canon dealing with the crime of apostasy.

Section II. Education of Youth in Communist Associations

In July of 1950, the Holy Office issued a *Monitum* regarding certain associations that have been formed by the Communists for the education of youth. It stated:

> Some associations have been set up, under the pressure and leadership, as everyone knows, of the Communist Party, which have for their purpose to imbue boys and girls with principles and training which are materialistic and contrary to Christian morality and faith.
>
> The faithful are therefore warned that such associations, whatever may be the name under which they disguise themselves, are subject to the sanctions mentioned in the Decree of the Holy Office issued on 1st of July, 1949.
>
> 1. Hence parents or those who stand in their place, who contrary to canon 1372, § 2 and the above mentioned Decree of the Holy Office, turn their children over to the aforesaid associations to be trained, cannot be admitted to the reception of the sacraments.
> 2. Those who teach boys and girls what is contrary to faith and to Christian morals incur an excommunication specially reserved to the Holy See.
> 3. The boys and girls themselves, as long as they have part in these associations, cannot be admitted to the sacraments.[268]

It was seen in the first chapter,[269] that one of the first steps

[268] *AAS,* XXXXII (1950), 553; *Digest,* III, 660-661.

[269] Cf. *supra,* pp. 34-38.

the Party takes when it sets up operations in a country is to establish a network of Front Organizations. The purposes of these groups vary from one country to the next, depending largely on the local objectives and needs of the Party. It was also seen that these groups are frequently organized for particular classes of people, lawyers, writers, teachers, etc. These associations mentioned in the *Monitum* of 1950 are perfect examples of Front Organizations established for the youth.

It will help to recall, too, that the Party generally prefers to have its relationship with these various groups remain hidden. For that reason, characteristically the Fronts operate under titles and purported plans which ostensibly in no way suggest their association with the Party. The Holy Office, well aware of this technique, warns the faithful in this *Monitum* that the sanctions apply to such associations regardless of what names they use to disguise themselves.[270] Although these associations for the education of youth are not generally employed by the Party in the United States, great use has been made of them in certain parts of Europe.[271]

It seems that these organizations are not primarily concerned with instructing the youth in the principles of Communism. Rather, the task of these associations seems to be one of preparing future generations for the reception of Communist philosophy. They are also obviously trying to eliminate possible future sources of resistance. This preparatory training, or softening-up process, consists in striving to inculcate into the youth of these countries the spirit of materialism and a disdain for the healthy and necessary restraints of religion and morality. In the words of the *Monitum* these associations have for their purpose "to imbue boys and girls with the principles and training which are materialistic and contrary to Christian morality."[272] It is well to recall that although these associations might not be using Marx's *Manifesto* for a text-

---

[270] Cf. *supra*, p. 128.

[271] E.g. in Italy the Party sponsors such groups as "The Youth Front," "The Union of Italian Girls," "The Association of Italian Pioneers." There are similar associations operating in countries behind the Iron Curtain—Cardini, "Adnotationes," *Monitor Ecclesiasticus*, LXXV (1950), 545-546.

[272] Cf. *supra*, p. 128.

book, or advocating the basic principles of Communism, these associations, nevertheless, are part of the Party's program to propagate the errors of Communism. Again, such associations cannot be isolated from the movement, since they are established by the Communists, operate under their direction and for ends fixed by the Party.

The *Monitum* warns the faithful that regardless of what names these associations operate under they are still subject to the sanctions of the Decree of 1949. It will be recalled that the first questions of that Decree asked whether it is licit to give one's name to the Parties of the Communists, or to favor them. The reply was in the negative.[273] In other words, the *Monitum* says that since these associations are set-up under the pressure and leadership of the Communists they must be considered as included in the term "Parties of the Communists" used by the Holy Office in its Decree of 1949. Therefore, it is not lawful to join these associations or to favor them. Secondly, it is forbidden to publish, propagate, or read books, daily papers, periodicals, etc., sponsored by these associations.[274] And finally, anyone who knowingly and freely does the above mentioned acts cannot be admitted to the sacraments.[275]

1) *Parents.* The *Monitum* states that parents, and those who take their place, who turn their children over to these associations to be educated are violating the command of canon 1372, § 2. This canon solemnly warns that not only on parents, in accordance with the norm of canon 1113, but also on all who stand in their place is there incumbent the right and the most serious duty to ensure the Christian education of the children. Moreover, as the

[273] *AAS,* XXXXI (1949), 334; *Digest,* III, 658. It should be noted here that the *Digest* translates the term used by the Holy Office, *"partibus communistarum"* as "Communist Party." It also does this in its translation of the *Monitum* of 1950, *ibid.,* p. 660. More properly, the term should be translated "Communist Parties."

[274] Cardini mentions three prominent magazines being produced by these organizations at the time of the *Monitum* (1950) : *Pioniere, Noi Ragazzi, Falco-Rosso, art. cit.,* 547; cf. *infra,* pp. 132-146 concerning Communist literature.

[275] Cf. *supra,* pp. 59-60, 128.

Monitum notes, parents who turn their children over to these associations to be trained are acting contrary to the Decree of the Holy Office issued in 1949, inasmuch as these parents are showing favor to the Communist movement.[276] And hence, such parents cannot be admitted to the sacraments since they are not properly disposed.[277]

2) *Boys and Girls.* The *Monitum* further directs that the boys and girls themselves, as long as they have part in these associations, are not to be admitted to the sacraments.[278] Fabregas, in his short commentary on the *Monitum,* says that the sacraments are denied these children not because they themselves are being punished for their participation in these associations which their parents compel them to attend, rather, they are refused the sacraments because it would be *"indecens indecorumque"* to admit them while they are frequenting such places.[279] Cardini, in his commentary on the *Monitum,* says that if a boy freely and knowingly attends the lectures given by the teachers in these associations, then he is placing himself in the proximate occasion of losing his faith and corrupting his morals.[280] As for the boy or girl who attends these associations unwillingly or unknowingly, whether or not the child should be admitted to the sacraments is a problem that must be solved according to the circumstances of each case.[281]

The reasons offered by these commentators for refusing the sacraments to the children who attend these associations are certainly valid reasons. However, both seem to overlook the fact

---

[276] The children attending these associations do not actually join them (*nomen dantes*). The *Monitum* says, "turn their children over to the aforesaid associations to be trained." If the children actually joined these associations which, according to the *Monitum,* are to be considered as falling under the term "Communist Parties" used in the Decree of 1949, then the parents, in virtue of canon 2230, would be subject to the censure of canon 2335.

[277] Cf. *supra,* p. 128.

[278] Cf. *supra,* p. 128.

[279] "Annotationes," *Periodica,* XXXIX (1950), 313.

[280] *Art. cit.,* p. 548. Apparently, the practice of encouraging children in these associations to engage in various types of immorality is commonplace, —*loc. cit.*

[281] *Loc. cit.*

that the children, by attending these associations are showing favor to the Communist movement.

3) *Teachers.* In n. 2 of the *Monitum* it is explicitly stated that those who teach boys and girls what is contrary to faith and morals incur an excommunication specially reserved to the Holy See.[282] This is a concrete application of the Decree of 1949. Under that Decree, the penalty of excommunication is incurred for professing, and especially for propagating, the anti-Christian doctrine of Communism.[283] It must be recognized that even though these associations might not be teaching the principles of Communism as such, their whole program, nevertheless, is designed to assist in the propagation of Communism. Hence, those who teach in these associations are, *de facto,* propagating the anti-Christian doctrine of Communism.

Section III. Publishing, Propagating and Reading Communist Literature

The second question of the Decree of 1949 of the Holy Office is directed at one of the chief means used by the Communist movement in spreading its pernicious errors, its literature. The Question treats of a number of acts which directly or indirectly assist in the dissemination of Communist doctrines. The Question asks:

> Whether it is licit to publish, propagate, or read books, periodicals, daily papers, or sheets which promote the doctrine or action of Communists, or to write in them.

The Holy Office replied: "In the negative: for they are forbidden *ipso iure* (cf. c. 1399 of the Code of Canon Law)."[284]

The Holy Office states that Communist literature is forbidden *ipso iure* by canon 1399. This is an extensive canon dealing with twelve separate categories of books and literature generally[285] that are forbidden by law. Although the Decree of the Holy Office

---

[282] Cf. *supra,* p. 128.

[283] Cf. *supra,* pp. 59-60.

[284] *AAS,* XXXI (1949), 334; *Digest,* III, 658-659.

[285] Cf. canon 1384, § 2.

does not specify under which of the categories Communist literature is to be classified, an examination of the canon reveals that a number of categories can apply to the various types of literature which the Party employs to promote its doctrine and action. Before examining these categories it is necessary to recall the basic principle of Communist tactics stressed in the first chapter, *adaptability.*[286] In so far as is possible, the Party adapts its propaganda to the types of people it is attempting to "convert." One form of propaganda will be geared for the intellectuals, another for the workers, another for the youth, and so on. As Pius XI said in speaking of Communist propaganda, "It is shrewdly adapted to the varying conditions of diverse people."[287] Hence, in some areas the Party literature will attempt to overthrow the foundations of religion. In countries behind the Iron Curtain great efforts are made by the Party to attract the Uniate Catholics into schism.[288] Nor is there any scarcity of books in which the Party sets forth its basic doctrines of materialism, its philosophy of history, society, and man. Communist literature advocating such principles and goals will fall under n. 2 of canon 1399 which forbids books of any writers whatever propagating heresy, schism or attempting to overthrow the foundations of religion.

It was seen in the previous section that the Party has organized numerous associations for the education of youth.[289] One of the purposes of these organizations is to encourage the young people to develop a disdain for the healthy restraints of religion and morality. The magazines and periodicals published in conjunction with these associations can readily be classified under n. 3 of canon 1399. This number forbids books dedicated to an assault on religion or good morals.

In the examination of the tactics employed by the Communists against the Church, especially behind the Iron Curtain, but not exclusively, it was seen in the first chapter[290] that the attacks are frequently directed against the hierarchy and the clergy in order

[286] Cf. *supra,* pp. 20-24.
[287] Encycl. *Divini Redemptoris, AAS,* XXIX (1937), 72.
[288] Cf. *supra,* pp. 62-64.
[289] Cf. *supra,* pp. 128-132.
[290] Cf. *supra,* pp. 26-28.

to separate them from the faithful. Newspapers, magazines, etc., publicizing such false, malicious assaults are comprehended under n. 6 of canon 1399. This number prohibits books which, among other things, endeavor to undermine ecclesiastical discipline, or that are designed to cast opprobrium on the ecclesiastical hierarchy or on the clerical or religious state.

Finally, n. 8 of canon 1399 can conceivably be applied to a large amount of Communist literature. According to this number, books which argue that the Masons or other similar societies are useful or not pernicious in regard to the Church or the state are forbidden.[291] Even though this number requires some attempt at demonstration (*contendunt*), assuredly, many of the Communist books and magazines and newspapers satisfy this requisite.

In this whole question of Communist literature it is necessary to keep in mind the basic techniques of the Party's propaganda. It was seen in the first chapter[292] that frequently the Party makes no mention of the true motives of the movement. More often it concentrates on local needs, and points up the problems, contentions and inequalities existing among the people it is attempting to attract. Nor does it necessarily stress the connection between these so-called minor objectives and the final goal of the Party. One former Communist testified that 99 per cent of Communist propaganda had nothing to do with Communism.[293] Its immediate aim is to criticize the *status quo*. However, this method of attack is designedly part of the Communist program to promote the Communist doctrine and action. Hence although a given issue of a Communist newspaper or magazine may not seem to be prohibited by reason of the matter, the Church looks at the overall, cumulative effect of reading such publications. This is alluded to in the commentary of *L'Osservatore Romano* on the Decree of the Holy Office.

> But—say many—I only read the Communist paper to see what it says, to know all opinions: I have no wish

[291] Abbo-Hannan includes books defending Communism under this category. —*The Sacred Canons* (2 vols., St. Louis: B. Herder Co., 1951), II, 637.

[292] Cf. *supra*, pp. 32-34.

[293] Cf. *supra*, p. 33.

> whatever to profess materialism. Why forbid grown-ups to form their social and political opinions? We reply briefly. It is a fact that continual reading of these writings sooner or later brings confusion to the minds of the unexperienced people who are without adequate education, poisons the minds, puts their faith in danger, and is for many the cause of leaving the Church and abandoning religious practice.[294]

It is obvious that publishing, propagating and reading Communist literature, writing for magazines and newspapers and other publications promoting the movement can affect a person's canonico-juridical status. Although the Decree of the Holy Office merely states that a person who knowingly and freely performs these acts is to be refused the sacraments, actually, certain of these acts are subject to censure by the Code of Canon Law. However, before determining which acts are forbidden by censure, it will be well to set forth those that are forbidden under pain of sin.

A) Acts Forbidden Under Pain of Sin

The basic canon dealing with the effects of the prohibition of books is canon 1398. This canon states that the prohibition of books prescribes that without the required permission a book cannot be published, read, retained, sold, translated into another language, or in any way communicated to others.[295] However, before examining these acts in detail, it must be noted that although this canon speaks only of books and not of newspapers and periodicals, as does the Decree of the Holy Office, the canon that introduces this title on the censorship and prohibition of books must not be overlooked, namely, canon 1384, § 2. This canon provides that those things which are prescribed in this title in reference to books shall be applied, unless a contrary provision is clearly made, to daily and periodical publications, as well as to all other written publications whatever. Therefore, newspapers,

---

[294] *L'Osservatore Romano,* 27 July, 1949; translation from the *Tablet,* 6 Aug. 1949, 194, n. 5698, 87.

[295] Selling or communicating to others is comprehended by the term "propagate" used by the Decree of the Holy Office. Cf. *supra,* p. 132.

periodicals and brochures must be understood throughout this section, even though the term book is frequently employed.

1) *Publishing Forbidden Literature.* To publish (*edere*) a book means to cause a book to be multiplied and disseminated at one's own expense or at the expense of someone else.[296] This includes those who are the principal and primary cause of the publication among whom is certainly the publisher. The author is also included here if he submitted the work with the express intention of having it published.[297] Pernicone is of the opinion that more probably the printer as such is not comprehended by the term *edi* of canon 1398, § 1.[298] However, he cautions that it is always unlawful for a printer to give formal cooperation towards the production of a forbidden book. It is also wrong to give proximate material cooperation, except under certain circumstances.[299] The workers in the printing shop can also share in the guilt by cooperating in a lesser or greater degree towards the production of forbidden books.[300] However, most of these problems are not in the province of Canon Law.

Normally, a printed work is published. When the material is typewritten, mimeographed, handwritten, or the work is reproduced and multiplied by some similar means, the material is usually not intended for the general public, but for a restricted number of people, and therefore it is not considered published. But if by any of these means just mentioned, a work is made accessible to all indiscriminately, then that work, even though not printed, is considered published.[301]

2) *Reading a Forbidden Book.* One is said to read a book who, going over the book with his own eyes (or hands if he is blind),

---

[296] Pernicone, J., *The Ecclesiastical Prohibition of Books,* The Catholic University of America Canon Law Studies, n. 72 (Washington, D. C.: The Catholic University of America, 1932), p. 113.

[297] *Ibid.,* p. 114.

[298] *Loc. cit.*

[299] When this is permitted must be determined by the principles of moral theology.

[300] Vermeersch, *De Prohibitione et Censura Librorum,* p. 44.

[301] Pernicone, *op. cit.,* pp. 81-82. Moreover, the natural law is concerned with all writings, even those not published and forbids all which are dangerous, canon 1405, § 1.

understands what he reads. These two elements are essential to the definition of reading.[302] Therefore, it is not reading to listen to another read; nor can it be called reading to look over a book without knowing the language in which it is written. If, however, one knows the language of the book, but because of the difficulty of the subject matter treated, or the dullness of his mind, he does not fully understand the book, nevertheless he is reading in the sense just explained.

The law prohibiting the reading of forbidden books applies to all baptized persons[303] who are not exempted from the law.[304] The law includes even those who see no danger for themselves in reading a particular forbidden book, newspaper, periodical, etc. These laws on books are enacted to ward off the general danger of such writings and therefore bind even in individual cases in which the danger does not exist.[305]

Many of the authors discuss at length the amount of pages that must be read before one can be said to have read a forbidden book. Pernicone says that in practice reading only a few lines, even though of a very harmful nature, will not constitute grave legal matter. However, if a person reads six pages or more of a very harmful nature or thirty pages or more of a less serious character, this will constitute grave matter.[306]

3) *Keeping Forbidden Books.* A man is said to retain a book when he keeps it in his possession as his property. A person is also said to retain a book when he keeps it as a deposit or on loan.[307] If the owner of a forbidden book temporarily places the book in someone else's care, as long as he retains the ownership of the book he is said to retain the book.

It is also forbidden for any literary group, club or other organization of people to keep forbidden books without permission,

---

[302] Pernicone, *op. cit.*, p. 115.

[303] Cf. canon 87.

[304] Canon 1401 exempts Cardinals, bishops, also titulars, and ordinaries from the law regarding the prohibition of books.

[305] Cf. canon 21. Also, priests, teachers, etc. are not excepted.

[306] *Op. cit.*, p. 234.

[307] Ayrinhac, *Administrative Legislation in the New Code of Canon Law* (New York: Longmans, Green and Co., 1930), p. 291.

because the members of these associations are actually co-owners and possessors of the books, and hence they retain the books.[308] A librarian, however, does not *retain* the books committed to his care.[309] Bookbinders, too, are usually not considered as *retainers* of books since they normally only keep them until they are bound.

The prohibition against keeping forbidden literature applies to restaurants, hotels, barber shops and other such places where books, magazines and newspapers are placed at the disposal of customers. This has practical application with regard to Communist newspapers and magazines. It should be noted, however, that the employees of such places just mentioned are not considered the *retainers* of forbidden literature since they do not keep it in their own name.

Finally, in the question of keeping forbidden literature, whether or not the person retaining the book understands the language in which the book is written is of no importance. It is the *retaining* of the book that is forbidden. Some authors consider it grave matter to retain a forbidden book for more than two or three days, unless there is a reasonable cause to justify a longer delay.[310] Others, however, allow at least a month.[311]

4) *Selling Forbidden Literature.* Booksellers may not sell prohibited literature unless they have permission from the Apostolic See, and they shall not sell this literature to anyone unless they can prudently reach a decision that they are lawfully requested by the buyer.[312] Hence, they need not ask each customer whether or not he has permission to read said literature. The booksellers can make a prudent judgment from the nature of the book and the character of the buyer.[313]

It is reported that Cardinal Ruffini, Archbishop of Palermo, shortly after the Decree issued by the Holy Office in 1949, posed a question to the Holy Office regarding the position of certain

---

[308] Cappello, *De Censuris,* pp. 206-207.
[309] *Loc. cit.*
[310] Vermeersch, *op. cit.,* p. 102.
[311] Cappello, *op. cit.,* p. 206.
[312] Canon 1404.
[313] Pernicone, *op. cit.,* p. 119.

newsdealers in the light of the prohibition against selling Communist literature.[314] It seems in some countries, particularly in Italy, newsdealers are bound by union regulations to carry all registered publications. If they refuse to comply, their licenses can be revoked.[315] It is reported that the Holy Office responded to the question concerning the position of said newsdealers, that if they find themselves under this effective coercion of the union, material cooperation can be tolerated.[316] However, the cooperation should be as limited as possible.

5) *Translating and Communicating Forbidden Literature.* Translating a forbidden work is not permitted because the danger of a book consists not in the language in which it is written but in the matter which it contains. Therefore, the danger usually exists regardless of the language in which the book is written. However, if one has permission to read a prohibited book he may make a translation of the work for his own use.[317]

Communicating forbidden literature to others is forbidden and

---

[314] There is no mention in the *Acta* of the Cardinal's question, or the response of the Holy Office. However, they are mentioned by Sirna in his "Annotationes ad Decretum S. Officii de Communismo, "*Apollinaris*, XXII (1949), 62, n. 8. They are also given by Palazzini, *Casus Conscientiae* (3 vols., Romae: Officium Libri Catholici, 1956), II, *De Censuris*, 45.

[315] *The Tablet*, 3 Dec., 1949, 194, n. 5715, 396.

[316] ". . . In alcune città le organizzazioni sindacali, dalle quali dipendono le modalità di distribuzione dei giornali presso i chiosochi di rivendita, insistono con estremo vigore sull'obbligo dei giornalai di non escludere dalle loro rivendite questo o quel giornale, sotto pena di vedersi negata la consegna di tutti gli altri giornali.

"In altre città invece, i rivenditori possono senza difficoltà sottrarsi a tale imposizione. È chiaro che se il giornalaio può, senza suo grave danno, evitare la vendita dei giornali proibiti, tale rivenditore, se non si attiene alle disposizioni del noto Decreto del S. Offizio, pone 'scienter et libere' gli atti per i quali sono comminate le note sanzioni.

"Che se, invece, il giornalaio trovasi sotto la coazione effettiva dei suddetti sindacati, la sua cooperazione materiale può essere tollerata, fermo tuttavia restando sempre l'obbligo in coscienza di limitare quanto più è possibile tale cooperazione; ciò che può essere fatto con le piccole industrie, in cui gli stessi giornalai sono esperti, e che non è d'uopo qui elencare."—Cf. Sirna, *art. cit., loc. cit.;* cf. also Palazzini, *op. cit., loc. cit.*

[317] Pernicone, *op. cit.*, p. 120.

this includes lending, donating, exchanging, showing to others, reading or transcribing to others.[318]

6) *Writing for the Communists.* Although canon 1398 does not forbid writing for the Communists, the Decree of the Holy Office specifically states that it is illicit to write in books, newspapers, periodicals or sheets which promote the doctrine or action of Communists.[319] Since the Decree of the Holy Office does not specify a particular type of writing, all writing is forbidden even though it does not *per se* deal with questions of faith or morals.[320] Hence, it is not permitted to contribute articles dealing with such matters as literature, art, music, the theater, sports, etc. The reason for prohibiting even articles of this nature is given by the commentary on the Decree which appeared in *L'Osservatore Romano.* Such articles are prohibited, the commentary states, because the authors are thereby putting their talents and reputation at the service of the Party.[321] In other words, such acts amount to showing favor to the Communist movement.[322] Since these involve *cooperatio,* their gravity as well as the circumstances in which such acts may be tolerated must be solved according to the principles of moral theology.

Finally, although it has just been seen that publishing, selling, and communicating Communist literature is forbidden under pain of sin, it must be recalled that these acts are *de facto* assisting in the propagation of Communism. Therefore, under certain circumstances canon 2316 can be operable. Moreover, it is easy to imagine circumstances when these acts will place a person under n. 4 of the Decree of 1949. For example, one who writes articles in a Communist newspaper in which he attempts to defend the philosophy and program of Communism is certainly propagating and defending Communism in the sense of n. 4 of the Decree.[323]

---

[318] Teachers or professors who have the necessary permission to read prohibited books may read short excerpts of such works to their students when it is deemed necessary.—Pernicone, *op. cit.,* p. 120, n. 38.

[319] Cf. *supra,* p. 132.

[320] "Ubi lex non distinguit nec nos distinguere debemus."

[321] *Art. cit., loc. cit.*

[322] The Holy Office in n. 1 of the Decree issued in 1949 declared that it was illicit to show favor to the Communists. Cf. *supra,* p. 122.

[323] Cf. *supra,* p. 122.

B) Acts Forbidden Under Pain of Censure

When treating the subject of Communist literature, the Decree of the Holy Office merely states that the sacraments are not to be administered to those who publish, propagate, or read books, periodicals, daily newspapers, or sheets which promote the doctrine or action of Communists. Similarly, the sacraments are not to be administered to those who write in these works.[324] Although the Holy Office makes no mention of a censure here, when canon 2318, § 1 is examined, it is at once evident that some of these acts mentioned by the Decree can, under certain conditions, be delictual. Canon 2318, § 1 imposes an *ipso facto* excommunication specially reserved to the Holy See on those who publish books of apostates, heretics or schismatics which advocate their doctrines. The canon further states that the same penalty is incurred by those who defend or knowingly (*scienter*) and without the necessary permission read or retain these books. Hence, if a Catholic who professes Communism writes and causes to be published a book in which he advocates the errors of Communism, then that person, as well as the book, fall within the purview of canon 2318, § 1.[325] Therefore, consideration must be given to this canon to determine its scope and meaning, since a penalty established in law is not incurred unless the delict in question be perfect in kind according to the proper meaning of the words of the law.[326]

1) *Book.* The first condition that must be fulfilled before the penalty of this canon is incurred is that the book written by an apostate must be a book in the strictest sense of the word.[327] By a book is meant a volume of considerable size, having a certain unity of subject, or at least of tendency.[328] As to the size of a book, authors generally accept the figures of Schmalzgrueber, namely, 10 folio pages or 160 pages in *octavo* (the average book

---

[324] Cf. *supra*, p.

[325] A Catholic who professes Communism is an apostate, cf. *supra*, pp. 71-72, also, cf. *supra*, p. 136, for notion of *edere*.

[326] Canon 2228.

[327] Canon 19.

[328] Pernicone, *op. cit.*, p. 78.

page) or 320 pages in 16mo.[329] This element must not be judged mathematically but morally, together with the element of unity of subject or tendency.[330] Therefore, it can be said that the following types of Communistic literature are not comprehended in the provisions of canon 2318, § 1 by reason of the fact that they are not books in the strict sense of the word: booklets, pamphlets, newspapers, leaflets, etc. Authors do not agree on whether or not periodicals, reviews and magazines are comprehended in this canon. Pernicone says that the better opinion holds that these are not considered books in the strict sense of the word, even though they are bound in volumes. However, if the bound volume has the unity of subject, or at least, of tendency then it possibly could fall under this canon. The same can be said for booklets. However, the other conditions of the canon must be fulfilled, for example, the authors of the articles in the magazine must be apostates.[331] In practice, Pernicone says, very often periodicals, magazines, and reviews will escape the penalty.[332]

Anthologies, readers, historical source books or other similar works containing selections taken from the books of apostates, heretics, or schismatics in which their errors are noticeably propounded, are all forbidden under pain of excommunication as long as they retain those objectionable parts, and provided they have the unity of subject or tendency required to make a book in the strict sense.[333]

2) *Concerning the Author.* The second condition required by canon 2318, § 1 is that the book must be the work of an apostate, heretic or schismatic. Therefore, a book advocating the errors of Communism, written by a person who was never baptized does not come under this canon, since the author is not an apostate. However, the book is certainly forbidden.[334]

---

[329] *Ius Ecclesiasticum Universum,* V, pars prima, tit. VII, n. 55; Pernicone, *op. cit.,* pp. 79, 222.

[330] Pernicone, *op. cit.,* p. 222.

[331] Cf. *infra.*

[332] Pernicone, *op. cit.,* p. 224.

[333] Cf. *ibid.,* p. 226.

[334] The words *"Libri quorumvis scriptorum"* of canon 1399, 2° refer to baptized and non-baptized; cf. Pernicone, *op. cit.,* p. 135.

It is important to note that the author must advocate or defend Communism in the book before the work will be considered as falling under this canon. Hence, a book in which the author simply denies a doctrine of the faith, or ridicules it, or makes an occasional attack against the faith is not a book advocating apostasy or heresy.[335]

3) *Publishing Books of Apostates.* The notion of publication (*edere*) has already been treated.[336] It suffices to call to mind that the only person or group of persons who publish the work in their own name are publishers. The author and the printer as such are not publishers,[337] nor are the editors by canon 19, and canon 2219, § 1. However, if they (the author, printer, and editor) were accomplices with full responsibility for the publication of the work, or if the work would not have been published without their co-operation, they incur the same censure as the publishers.[338]

4) *Defending Books by Apostates.* A book can be defended in either of two ways. A person can hide a book or prevent it from being denounced or destroyed. More commonly, however, a book is defended by words or actions or writings which are designed to show that the doctrine in the book is sound and acceptable, or that the book should not be forbidden.[339] No censure is incurred by one who praises the style, the language or the literary qualities of the book, provided this is not done to commend the work.[340]

5) *Reading Books by Apostates.* The basic notion of reading has already been discussed.[341] To incur the penalty for reading

---

[335] Pernicone, *op. cit.,* p. 226.

[336] Cf. *supra,* p. 136.

[337] Cappello, *De Censuris,* p. 201, n. 225.

[338] Canons 2209, §§ 1-3, and 2231; cf. Pernicone, *op. cit.,* p. 229.

[339] Cf. Pernicone, *op. cit.,* p. 230. In connection with defending books by apostates, it should be noted that according to the Decree of the Holy Office, those who profess the anti-Christian doctrine of Communism, and especially those who defend it, incur an *ipso facto* excommunication. This is mentioned in n. 4 of that Decree, cf. *supra,* p. 72. To incur this penalty, however, that is, for defending Communistic errors put forth in a book, it is not required that the book be written by an apostate. The crime, in this case, is that of defending Communism, cf. *supra,* pp. 78-79.

[340] Vermeersch-Creusen, *Epitome Iuris Canonici,* III, 318.

[341] Cf. *supra,* pp. 136-137.

a book that falls under canon 2318, § 1, the person must know that the book in question was written by an apostate, and that the author advocates Communist errors in the book. Moreover, the person must know that the reading of such a book is forbidden under censure. Since canon 2318, § 1 requires that the reader act with perfect *dolus,*[342] ignorance of the law, the fact, or the penalty, even though the ignorance is crass, excuses from the penalty.[343]

It must be cautioned, however, that the legislator uses the word *"scienter"* only in conjunction with the acts of reading and retaining these books written by apostates. Therefore, if the publishers and defenders of books forbidden in this canon violate the law through crass or supine ignorance, they incur the penalty.[344]

6) *Retaining Books by Apostates.* The excommunication imposed on those who retain the books mentioned in canon 2318, § 1 generally does not apply to librarians, bookbinders, and employees who keep books for those who employ them.[345] However, the penalty can be incurred by booksellers who keep these books for public or private sale. Hence, if the bookseller keeps these books to sell to those who have permission to read them, he himself must have permission to retain these books, and he must not keep them open to public view, that is, on display.[346]

7) *"Opere Publici Iuris Facto."* The final condition that must be fulfilled before a person incurs the excommunication provided in canon 2318, § 1, is that the book comprehended by this law must have been put on sale or offered for public circulation (*opere publici facto*). Therefore, no one is affected by the censure in this canon if only a few copies of the work are printed, or if a large number of copies are printed not for general distribution but for a restricted number of persons (e.g., students of a professor). Nor would the penalty be incurred if all the printed copies of a

---

[342] Canon 2318, § 1 employs the word *"scienter"* in reference to reading and retaining the books described in the canon.

[343] Canon 2229, §§ 1 and 2.

[344] Canon 2229, § 3, 1°.

[345] Cf. *supra,* pp. 137-138, for notion of retaining books.

[346] Canon 1404; cf. canon 1398.

work intended for publication are destroyed before they are published. The same would be true if a prohibition of public authorities prevented the books from being distributed for sale. In short, the publishers, defenders, the readers or those who retain the books mentioned in this canon are not under excommunication unless the book has been published.[347]

Finally, the permission spoken of in this canon is treated in canon 247, § 4, and canon 1402.

---

[347] Pernicone, *op. cit.*, p. 233.

CHAPTER IV

Practical Conclusions

INTRODUCTION

Those who associate themselves with the Communist movement were divided, in the previous chapter, into three general groups: those who profess the errors of Communism; those who merely join the Communist Party; and those who in some way show favor to the Communist movement. Having determined the canonico-juridical status of people who fall into any one of these categories, it remains to consider in a general fashion some of the canonico-juridical effects that result from the profession of Communism, joining the Party or showing favor to the movement. In a word, the following are but practical conclusions that necessarily flow from the considerations presented in the previous chapter.

ARTICLE 1. THOSE WHO PROFESS COMMUNISM

It is seen that Catholics who profess the errors of Communism are considered as apostates and hence subject to the penalty of excommunication.[1] Canon 2257 defines the penalty of excommunication as: "... *censura qua quis excluditur a communione fidelium cum effectibus qui in canonibus, qui sequuntur, enumerantur, quique separari nequeunt.*" The nine canons which follow canon 2258 may roughly be divided into two categories. The first category treats of certain deprivations in the delinquent's own religious life. The second category deals with certain deprivations in the official ministrations to the religious life of others.

Before setting forth some of these effects of the censure of excommunication, it is well to recall the provision of the law which is

[1] Cf. *supra*, p. 72. Those who teach in the Communist associations organized for the education of youth also fall into this category; cf. *supra*, p. 132.

stated in canon 2232, § 1. This canon directs that a *latae sententiae* penalty, whether medicinal or vindicative, binds the delinquent in the external forum and the internal forum, if he is conscious of the crime. It further provides that before a declaratory sentence is pronounced the delinquent is excused from the observance of the penalty whenever he cannot observe it without defaming himself. Moreover, in the external forum, the canon continues, no one can demand its observance of him unless the crime is notorious, without prejudice to the provisions of canon 2223, § 4.

By way of summary, it can be said that no one who has incurred a latae sententiae penalty is obliged to observe the penalty unless one of the following conditions is verified:

1) unless a declaratory sentence has been issued
2) unless the delict is notorious
3) unless the delinquent can observe the penalty without loss of reputation

It is well to keep this benign provision of the law in mind when considering the following canonical, juridical effects of the censure of excommunication.

Section I. Assistance at Divine Offices

Every excommunicated person lacks the right to assist at any divine service with the exception of the preaching of the word of God.[2] If the delinquent is an *excommunicatus toleratus,* it is not required that he be expelled if he assists passively.[3] But if he is an *excommunicatus vitandus* he must be expelled, or if expulsion is not possible, the service must be terminated, if this can be done without serious inconvenience. Moreover, not only the latter, but also any other whose excommunication has been the subject of a declaratory or a condemnatory sentence or has otherwise become notorious must be excluded from the active assistance at divine services.[4]

---

[2] Canon 2259, § 1.
[3] Canon 2259, § 2.
[4] *Can. cit.*

Section II. Participation in the Common Suffrages of the Church

Excommunicated persons do not partake of the indulgences, suffrages, and public prayers of the Church.[5] However, it is not forbidden to pray for them privately, and Masses may be offered for them privately in the absence of scandal.[6] But if the excommunicated is a *vitandus,* Mass may be offered only for his conversion.[7]

Section III. Exercising Legitimate Ecclesiastical Acts

An excommunicated person is excluded from the exercise of legitimate ecclesiastical acts within the limits set in the respective norms of the law. He cannot enter suit in an ecclesiastical court except as is allowed in canon 1654. He is forbidden to hold any ecclesiastical office or post or to enjoy privileges granted him prior to his excommunication.[8]

The question of sponsorship at Baptism and Confirmation should be given special attention. Canons 765 and 795 state that those excommunicated by a declaratory or condemnatory sentence cannot validly act as sponsors. Canon 766 and canon 796 state that those who are guilty of a notorious delict cannot licitly act as sponsors.

Canons 766 and 796 imply that occult excommunicates can licitly be *admitted* as sponsors. It is to be noted that both of these canons speak of those who may be *admitted* as sponsors. These canons do not treat of those who may *act* as sponsors. Certainly a person who is excluded from legitimate ecclesiastical acts, even for a delict that is not notorious, *per se* cannot act licitly as a sponsor. Nor can it be said that an excommunicate has a right to act as sponsor.[9] But if a person's crime of professing Communism is occult, he may be *admitted* as a sponsor at Baptism or Confirmation, which is in conformity with canon 2232.[10] How-

---

[5] Canon 2262, § 1.

[6] Canon 2262, § 2, 1°-2°.

[7] Canon 2262, § 2, 2°.

[8] Canon 2263.

[9] Canon 2259, § 1: "Excommunicatus quilibet caret iure assistendi divinis officiis. . . ."

[10] Hyland, F., *Excommunication, Its Nature, Historical Development and Effects,* The Catholic University of America Canon Law Studies, n. 49 (Washington, D. C.: The Catholic University of America, 1928), p. 133.

ever, it was stated in the third chapter that if a given Communist Party professes atheism as its proper, anti-religious doctrine and maintains atheism as its proper doctrinal system, and its primary end, then joining that Party or publicly adhering to it begets *infamia iuris.*[11] Hence, such a person cannot validly act as a sponsor at Baptism or Confirmation.[12]

In case of doubt as to whether or not a person is to be admitted as a sponsor, recourse must be had to the Ordinary, if time permits.[13]

Section IV. Reception of the Sacraments

In keeping with the purpose of this chapter, namely, to consider in a general way the canonical effects of excommunication, only what seem to be the more pertinent points will be considered here. For a more detailed study the authors and commentators must be consulted.

A) Baptism

If an unbaptized person has professed the errors of Communism and now desires to enter the Church, he is admitted to the Fold through the reception of the sacrament of Baptism. Neither the abjuration of former errors, nor the absolution from censures or sins is required.[14] There is no need for absolution from censures, since only subjects of the Church are capable of incurring censures.[15] If a doubtfully baptized person has professed Communism, repents and wishes to enter the Church, he is received according to the following procedure:

1) Abjuration or Profession of Faith
2) Conditional Baptism
3) Sacramental Confession and conditional absolution.[16]

[11] Cf. *supra,* pp. 120-121.

[12] Canons 765, 2° and 795, 2°.

[13] Canon 767.

[14] Goodwine, J., *The Reception of Converts,* The Catholic University of America Canon Law Studies, n. 198 (Washington, D. C.: The Catholic University of America Press, 1944), p. 55. This author notes, however, that in England the profession of faith is required.

[15] Cf. *supra,* p. 73.

[16] S.C.S. Off., instr., 20 Iul. 1859—*Fontes,* IV, n. 953.

If parents who profess Communism present their child for baptism (this is not altogether unlikely), the regulation of canon 750, § 2 must be followed. That is, there must be sufficient guaranty that the child will receive a Catholic education.

B) Holy Communion

If the person's delict of professing Communism is public, he is to be denied Holy Communion whether he petitions to receive the Sacrament publicly or in secret.[17] If the delict is occult, he is to be denied the Sacrament if he petitions in secret and the minister knows the delinquent has not repented.[18] However, if the same delinquent publicly petitions to receive Holy Communion, the minister must not pass him by if this cannot be done without scandal.[19]

C) Orders

Orders cannot licitly be conferred on one who professes Communism.[20] If a Catholic who had professed Communism, rejects his errors and upon return to the Church seeks admission to Orders, he must first be dispensed from the irregularity incurred by apostasy.[21] Under certain conditions, those who join or publicly adhere to a particular type of Communist Party are also irregular because they have become infamous (*infamia iuris*).[22]

If a person who has never been baptized, abandons the profession of Communism, enters the Church and seeks admission to Orders, consideration must be given to the impediment mentioned in canon 987, 6°. That is, those who are neophytes, until, in the

---

[17] Canon 855, § 1.

[18] Canon 855, § 2.

[19] *Can. cit.*

[20] Canon 2260, § 1; cf. also canons 2265, § 1, 3°, and 2374.

[21] Canon 985, 1°; canon 968, § 1; cf. also canon 990 regarding the power to dispense from occult delicts.

[22] Canon 984, 5°. Cf. *supra*, pp. 114-121, for the conditions that must be fulfilled before one who joins or publicly adheres to a Communist Party will be considered to have become infamous.

judgment of the Ordinary, they have been sufficiently tried, are simply impeded from orders.

A problem can arise if a son born of professed Communists seeks ordination. According to canon 987, 1° such a person labors under a simple impediment. However, if the parents are converted prior to his ordination, then the son is freed from the impediment.[23] However, as long as one of the parents remains a professed Communist, which status he had at the time of his son's birth, the son may not receive ordination unless a dispensation is obtained.[24] If the parents were professed Communists at the time of the birth of the son, and then later became converts to the true faith, but still later, prior to the ordination of the son, lapse into Communism, the son does not fall under the prohibition of canon 987, 1°.[25] In other words, if at any time after the son's birth both of his parents have been Catholics, then the impediment of canon 987, 1° will thereafter no longer exist.[26]

D) Matrimony

Because the Holy Office has issued a special decree concerning the marriage of Communists, more consideration must be given to that sacrament.[27]

The Holy Office was asked whether the exclusion from the use of the Sacraments, prescribed by the Decree of the Holy Office of July 1, 1949, implies also exclusion from the celebration of marriage; and if not, whether the marriages of Communists are governed by the provisions of canons 1060-1061.

The Holy Office declared that, in view of the special nature of marriage, the priest can assist at the marriages of Communists according to canon 1065 and 1066. Among other things, these canons

[23] Canon 987, 1° says: ". . . quandi parentes in suo errore permanent."

[24] Cf. *AAS*, XI (1919), 478; *Digest*, I, 487.

[25] Cf. Vogelpohl, H., *The Simple Impediments to Holy Orders*, The Catholic University of America Canon Law Studies, n. 224 (Washington, D. C.: The Catholic University of America Press, 1945), pp. 136-137.

[26] *Loc. cit.; permanent* supposes a continued action or status.

[27] *AAS*, XXXXI (1949), 427; cf. *Digest*, III, 407-408; cf. *supra*, p. 60 for text.

require the permission of the Ordinary before the marriage can take place.

The Holy Office further stated, however, that in the marriages of the persons referred to in n. 4 of the Decree of 1949 (that is, those of the faithful who profess Communism) the provisions of canons 1061, 1102, and 1109, § 3 are to be followed.

It must be recalled that in this section consideration is being given only to those who profess Communism. The marriages of those who simply join the Party or those who show favor to Communism are treated in the next section.[28]

Canon 1061 mentioned in the Decree of the Holy Office regarding the marriages of those who profess Communism, states the conditions that must be fulfilled before a dispensation *mixtae religionis* will be granted. Canon 1102 requires that in marriage between a Catholic and a non-Catholic party the questions requiring an expression of consent must be put in accordance with canon 1095, § 1, 3°. It further states that all sacred rites are forbidden, but it gives the Ordinary the power to permit some of the usual ecclesiastical ceremonies. Finally, canon 1109, § 3 legislates concerning the place where marriages between a Catholic and a non-Catholic party are to take place.

From these canons cited by the Holy Office it might be concluded that the marriage between a Catholic and one of the faithful who has abandoned the faith and is professing Communism is a mixed marriage. However, such a conclusion is not correct, as is clearly shown by Cardinal Ottaviani in his commentary on the Decree of the Holy Office regarding the marriages of Communists.[29] Briefly, the reasons are as follows:

First, a mixed marriage is described in canon 1060 as a marriage between two baptized persons one of whom is a Catholic while the other is affiliated with a heretical or schismatical sect. Now it is true that the Pontifical Commission for the Authentic Interpretation of the Code of Canon Law in 1934 decreed that members of atheistic sects are to be considered as regards all legal effects, even Sacred Ordination and marriage, the same as persons

---

[28] Cf. *infra*, pp. 165-167.

[29] "De Communistarum Matrimoniis," *Apollinaris*, XXII (1949), 101-105.

who belong or have belonged to a non-Catholic sect.[30] However, Cardinal Ottaviani points out, as has been done in this work in a previous section,[31] that *per se* the Communist Party is not an atheistic sect in the sense of the Decree of 1934.[32] If in a given country, however, the Party does qualify as an atheistic sect,[33] then a marriage between a Catholic and a Communist enrolled in such a sect will require a dispensation *mixtae religionis,* not by force of the Decree of the Holy Office of 1949, but by reason of the interpretation of 1934.[34]

Secondly, to establish the fact that the marriage between a Catholic and one of the faithful who professes Communism is not a mixed marriage, *per se,* the Cardinal calls attention to the wording of the Decree of the Holy Office concerning these marriages. He notes that the Decree significantly omits any mention of canon 1060 in replying to the question whether or not these marriages are governed by canons 1060-1061.[35] The Holy Office says that the marriages of those who profess Communism are governed by canons 1061, 1102, and 1109, § 3. If such marriages were mixed marriages, it would have been sufficient to state that the marriages of those who profess Communism are impeded by canon 1060. It would not have been necessary to mention canon 1061.[36] It should be noted that a person can profess Communism without ever belonging to the Communist Party.

The conclusion, therefore, is that a marriage between a Catholic and one of the faithful who professes Communism is not, *per se,* a mixed marriage, and hence no dispensation is required.[37]

---

[30] *AAS,* XXVI (1934), 494; cf. *Digest,* II, 286-287.

[31] Cf. *supra,* pp. 114-121.

[32] *Art. cit.,* p. 103.

[33] Cf. *supra,* pp. 120-121.

[34] *Art. cit.,* p. 103.

[35] *Art. cit., loc. cit.*

[36] *Loc. cit.*

[37] This opinion is also held by Sirna, "Annotationes ad Decretum S. Officii de Comm.," *Apollinaris,* XXII (1949), 68; Bidagor, "Adnotationes," *Monitor Ecclesiasticus,* LXXIV (1949), 55; Fagiolo, "Consultationes," *Monitor Ecclesiasticus,* LXXV (1950), 480; Conway, however, holds it is a mixed marriage, "The Decree of the Holy Office on Communism," *The Irish Ecclesiastical Record,* LXXIII, 65.

However, the marriage must be treated like a mixed marriage and therefore the Ordinary must be consulted. The Ordinary, after an examination of all the circumstances, may permit the priest to assist at the marriage, provided a serious reason exists for this, and the Ordinary in a prudent decision judges that there is sufficient guaranty of the exclusive Catholic education of the offspring and a removal of the danger of perversion of the other spouse.[38]

Moreover, all the sacred rites are forbidden. But if it is foreseen that from this prohibition greater evils will follow, the Ordinary can permit some of the usual ecclesiastical ceremonies, but never the celebration of Mass.[39] The marriage is not to be held in church, unless the Ordinary shall prudently judge that this provision cannot be observed because greater evils will result.[40]

E) Extreme Unction

This sacrament shall not be administered to those who contumaciously remain impenitent in manifest mortal sin. But if there is a doubt in regard to this state, it should be conferred conditionally.[41] Administration of this sacrament to those destitute of their senses is governed by canon 943.[42]

Section V. Administration of the Sacraments

According to canon 2261, an excommunicate, whether *vitandus*

---

[38] Canon 1061. Canons 1065-1066 are applicable in cases of notoriety and publicity. But in practice such a case is also attended to under the application and prescript of canon 1061.

[39] Canon 1102.

[40] Canon 1109, § 3.

[41] Canon 942. Kilker discusses the various opinions of authors concerning the condition to be attached to the administration of the sacrament in these cases wherein it is doubtful whether or not the subject is contumaciously persevering in manifest mortal sin. He concludes that since the condition need not be expressed, it may be advisable for the priest simply to intend the bestowal of the sacrament *"ad mentem Ecclesiae,* or *"ad normam iuris."* —*Extreme Unction,* The Catholic University of America Canon Law Studies, n. 32 (Washington, D. C.: The Catholic University of America, 1926), pp. 245-247.

[42] Cf. *ibid.*, pp. 249-261.

or *toleratus,* is forbidden to celebrate Mass, to administer the sacraments and to prepare and administer the sacramentals. This canon has special application in countries behind the Iron Curtain where a number of priests have incurred excommunications for their activities with the Communists.[43]

However, like many rules, the regulation prohibiting the active use of the sacraments by those who are excommunicated has its exceptions. For example, the faithful, for any just reason, may request a *simpliciter toleratus* to administer the sacraments or sacramentals, especially when there are no other priests available.[44] Canon 2261, § 3 states under what conditions the faithful may request the administration of the sacraments and the sacramentals at the hands of the *vitandi* and the *tolerati* against whom a declaratory or condemnatory sentence has been passed. It states that the faithful, *only* when they are constituted in danger of death, may request such excommunicates to impart sacramental absolution in accordance with canons 882 and 2252, and also, if no other ministers are present, to administer the other sacraments and sacramentals.

Section VI. Reception of the Sacramentals

Canon 2260, § 1 directs that after a declaratory or condemnatory sentence an excommunicate cannot receive the sacramentals.[45] Canon 1152, however, declares that exorcisms can be pronounced over non-Catholics and excommunicates. As to blessings, canon 1149 says that they are intended primarily for Catholics. But the same canon adds that blessings may be given to non-Catholics for the purpose of obtaining the light of faith, and secondarily, the health of body. Since the Catholic who professes Communism and the baptized non-Catholic are presumed to be equally guilty of their heretical depravity,[46] it would seem there is no reason to deny the

---

[43] Cf. *supra*, pp. 64-66.

[44] Canon 2261, § 2; cf. also, canon 2232, § 1.

[45] Hyland says that there is a distinction between the reception and use of sacramentals and maintains that this canon prohibits the reception, not the use.—*Op. cit.*, pp. 79-80.

[46] Canon 2200, § 2.

former what is allowed the latter.[47] Scandal, of course, must be avoided.

Section VII. Privation of Ecclesiastical Burial

Canon 2260, the canon which sets forth the general prohibition against the reception of the sacraments and sacramental by those excommunicated, states that in regard to ecclesiastical burial the prescription of canon 1240, § 1, 2° is to be followed. This canon directs that notorious apostates are to be denied ecclesiastical burial. Since the canon demands that the act of apostasy be notorious, the person's apostasy must be so certain as to the fact and the guilt that it can in no way be concealed or excused, or both the act and the wrong intention be so apparent to the people that there is no room left for even a slight doubt about either.[48] Therefore, before a person who professes Communism can be denied a Christian burial, his delict must be notorious. Moreover, the canon generously grants that if there has been any sign of repentance, ecclesiastical burial may be permitted. If a doubt should arise in regard to the application of this law, the Ordinary shall be consulted, time permitting. If the doubt persists, the body of the deceased shall be given Christian burial, in such a way, however, as to prevent scandal.[49]

Section VIII. Absolution

The mercy of the Church is well exemplified in canon 2314, § 2 which provides the method to be followed in absolving apostates. According to this canon absolution *in foro conscientiae* is reserved to the Holy See. However, if the case is brought in any way to the external forum of the Ordinary, this canon grants him (not the vicar general without a special mandate) the power to absolve in the external forum. Canon 2251 declares, moreover, that absolution which is granted in the external forum has effect in each forum. Hence, after the censure is absolved in the external forum,

---

[47] Cf. MacKenzie, p. 68.

[48] Canon 2197, 3°; cf. Kerin, *The Privation of Christian Burial,* p. 163.

[49] Canon 1240, § 2.

any confessor can absolve from the sin in the internal forum since absolution from the delict of apostasy in the internal forum is reserved *ratione censurae, not ratione peccati.* Once the censure is absolved then there is no further reservation of the sin. However, if absolution has been obtained only in the internal forum, though perfectly valid, it does not have effect in the external forum, unless it can be proved or legitimately presumed. However, if scandal is removed one who has obtained absolution in the internal forum may conduct himself as absolved in the external forum.

In danger of death any priest, although not approved for confessions, can licitly and validly absolve from all censures.[50] Moreover, canon 2254 gives confessors faculties to absolve from censures in certain more urgent cases.[51]

These, it is felt, are some of the more practical conclusions incident to the profession of Communism.

ARTICLE 2. THOSE WHO JOIN THE COMMUNIST PARTY

Basically, the canonico-juridical position of a person who joins the Communist Party is the same as one who professes Communism. Both crimes are punished by excommunication.[52] Hence, what was said in the previous article concerning the effects of the censure of excommunication apply, with certain modifications, to those who join the Communist Party. These modifications, or effects which are proper to the crime of joining the Communist Party, are the subject matter of the present article.

Section I. Clerics and Religious Who Join the Party

Since the Communist Party is the type of sect comprehended by Canon 2335, then the provisions of canon 2336 are applicable to the Party. Hence, clerics who join the Communist Party, in addition to the penalties provided in canon 2335, shall be punished either by suspension from or by deprivation of any benefice, office, dignity, pensions or position they may have in the Church; and

---

[50] Canon 882.

[51] Cf. also the Quinquennial Faculties granted to the Ordinaries of the United States,—*Digest,* Annual Supplement Through 1956, under canon 66.

[52] Cf. *supra,* pp. 71-72 and 85-108.

religious, by the privation of office and of active and passive voice, and by other penalties according to the constitutions. Moreover, clerics and religious who join the Communist Party are to be reported to the Sacred Congregation of the Holy Office.[53]

Section II. Admission to Associations of the Faithful

Canon 693, § 1 states that those who join condemned societies cannot validly be received into associations of the faithful. Quigley, tracing the interesting background to this portion of canon 693, finds the source of this law in two papal letters.[54] The first is a letter from Pius IX, *Quamquam Dolores,* written to Bishop Gonzales Oliveira, bishop of Olinda, Brazil.[55] The second is a constitution by the same pope to all the bishops of Brazil.[56] Both of these deal with the terrible outrages committed against the Church in Brazil by Masonic members of confraternities and third orders. Quigley notes that for many years prior to the great Masonic persecution of the Church in Brazil, it was only with the greatest difficulty that a person not a Mason could join a confraternity, e.g., of Mount Carmel, or the Third Order of St. Francis. "Masonic Catholics," infiltrated into these associations, gained control, and turned them against the Church.[57]

Hence, the present law of canon 693 was designed to prevent a recurrence of the tragedies that befell the Church in Brazil. According to canon 693, § 1 those who join condemned societies cannot validly be received in these associations of the faithful described in canon 685. These societies are: Third Orders Secular, Confraternities, and Pious Unions. Third Orders Secular are aggregations of secular tertiaries, who being in the world strive towards Christian perfection under the guidance of some order and according to its spirit.[58] Associations of the faithful erected for the exercise of works of piety or charity are called pious unions.[59] If pious unions are constituted after the manner of

[53] Canon 2336, § 2.
[54] *Condemned Societies,* pp. 89-93.
[55] Ep. *Quamquam Dolores,* 29 Maii, 1873—*Fontes,* III, n. 563.
[56] Ep. *Exortae,* 20 Apr. 1876—*Fontes,* III, n. 571.
[57] *Op. cit.,* pp. 89-90.
[58] Canon 702, § 1.
[59] Canon 707, § 1.

organized bodies they are called sodalities. Sodalities erected for the increase of public worship, e.g., the Children of Mary, are known under the specific name of confraternities.[60] All of these are comprehended by the term "association" used in canon 693, § 1.

It is to be noted that the person's joining the Communist Party need not be notorious, or even public. Hence, if one has joined the Party, even though the fact is not known, his admission to a pious association is invalid, and hence he cannot enjoy the rights and privileges of lawful members.

Section III. Entrance into the Novitiate

Canon 542, 1° says that those who have adhered to *"sectae acatholicae"* are invalidly admitted to the novitiate. In 1934 the Pontifical Commission for the Authentic Interpretation of the Code of Canon Law declared that those who joined atheistic sects are to be considered as regards all legal effects the same as persons who belong or have belonged to a non-Catholic sect.[61] From this it might seem that one who has belonged to the Communist Party cannot validly be admitted to the novitiate. However, it has been seen in the previous chapter that only under certain conditions will a Communist Party be considered an atheistic sect in the sense of the response of 1934.[62] Hence, it is the opinion of the writer that unless a person joins a Communist Party that is atheistic in the sense of the response of 1934, he can be validly admitted to the novitate.[63]

---

[60] Canon 707, § 2.

[61] *AAS,* XXVI (1934), 494; *Digest,* II, 286-287.

[62] Cf. *supra,* pp. 114-121 for conditions. Schaefer, commenting on this impediment, says: "Nomine sectae acatholicae non veniunt illae sectae, quae non sunt directe religiosae, etsi pluribus erroribus faveant et grave damnum Ecclesiae inferant; ex. gr. sectae massonicae, carbonariorum."—*De Religiosis ad Normam Codicis Iuris Canonici* (4. ed., Romae: Typis Polyglottis Vaticanis, 1940), p. 424.

[63] Cardinal Gasparri's index to the Code, under the title "Societates ab Ecclesia damnatae," says, "qui ad eas pertinent . . . admitti nequeunt in novitiatum."

Quigley says it is not clear what is meant by this since nowhere in canon 542 is it stated that members of condemned societies are invalidly or illicitly admitted to the novitiate.—*Op. cit.,* p. 107.

Section IV. Christian Burial

Canon 1240, § 1, 1° decrees that Ecclesiastical burial is to be denied to those notoriously addicted (*addicti*) to Masonic sects or other societies of the same nature. Since it has been determined that the Communist Party is a society similar to the Masons,[64] it follows that those who are *notorie addicti* to the Party are to be denied Christian burial.[65] The term *"addicti"* should not be limited to membership in the strict sense, since a person can be addicted to a society without being formally received as a member. The term can embrace those who frequent the meetings of the Party, or publicly defend the organization.[66] It is not the insertion of one's name (*nomen dans*) but public adherence to the sect that is of primary importance in the question of refusing burial. Ciprotti says that it is sufficient even if one is publicly accounted as a member of the sect.[67]

The Holy Office has declared that a person cannot be considered an occult Mason if he frequents Masonic meetings, if he wears their emblems and insignia publicly, and, in general, if he shows that he is a member of Masonry.[68] This norm is certainly applicable to the Communist Party, at least in certain countries where the Party permits its members to advertise their affiliation with the Party.

In short, it can be said that there need be no exact determination of how one became associated with the Communist Party. In the matter of Christian burial, it is the public appearance that counts.[69] However, it should be noted that in order to incur the penalty of the privation of Christian burial it is necessary that the person's addiction to the Party be notorious. Hence, he must appear in the eyes of the public to have known that his adherence was forbidden by the Church and to have chosen to adhere to the

---

[64] Cf. *supra*, pp. 85-108.

[65] Notorious is defined in canon 2197, 3°; cf. *infra*.

[66] Cf. Coronata, *Institutiones*, I, 709 for the meaning of *adhaesio*, which is similar to *addicti*.

[67] "De Consummatione Delicti," *Apollinaris*, VIII (1935), 233.

[68] S.C.C., Off., 27 Jun. 1838—*Fontes*, IV, n. 877.

[69] Kerin, *The Privation of Christian Burial*, p. 190.

Party despite the fact that this is forbidden. His crime must appear so blameworthy that no doubt exists.[70] It must also be remembered that if the delinquent has given some sign of repentance before death, he is not to be denied Christian burial.[71] In case of doubt, the matter must be referred to the Ordinary if time permits. If the doubt persists, the body may be given a Christian burial, provided scandal is not caused by this.[72] Scandal, however, as Kerin notes, must be avoided in all cases, not only in matters of doubt. This is enjoined by divine law itself.[73] For that reason, then, Christian burial must be denied when it is prudently foreseen that its concession will inevitably result in grave scandal for the faithful, regardless of the fact that the scandal is due to circumstances for which the deceased was not responsible.[74] Thus, if the family insists on displaying Communist banners and insignia (and this has been attempted on occasion), in such circumstances public order will override the right of the deceased and if grave scandal cannot be obviated, Christian burial must be denied.[75] However, in cases where the authorities judge grave harm will be done either to religion or to themselves if they refuse ecclesiastical burial to a deceased Communist, they may grant it, as long as it will not be construed as in contempt of religion.[76]

Section V. Absolution

If a confessor determines that a penitent has actually incurred the censure of canon 2335, and perhaps such cases will be rare, since many will be excused from the censure by reason of ig-

---

[70] *Ibid.*, p. 171.

[71] Canon 1240, § 1.

[72] Canon 1240, § 2.

[73] *Op. cit.*, p. 150.

[74] *Loc. cit.*

[75] Cf. *ibid.*, p. 151.

[76] Cf. Oietti, *Synopsis Rerum Moralium et Juris Pontificium* (4 vols., Romae: 1912), n. 3704. In this connection it is well to note the provision of canon 2339 concerning those who dare to command or coerce ecclesiastical authorities to grant Christian burial to those excommunicated. It is reported this has occurred in countries behind the Iron Curtain.

norance,[77] then recourse must be had to the Holy See.[78] However, in occult cases the law gives the Ordinary power to absolve.[79]

It will more frequently happen, however, that a person will have joined the Communist Party, realizing that such an act is gravely sinful, but totally ignorant of the fact that his act begets the censure of canon 2335. It is also very likely that in certain countries the faithful will join the Party because of moral or even physical force.

Ignorance of the law or the penalty or the fact can be claimed as an excusing cause if the ignorance is not crass or supine.[80] Fear, necessity or *incommodum,* if it is grave, can similarly be offered as an excusing cause provided the crime in question is not directed to contempt of faith, ecclesiastical authority, or work to the public detriment of souls.[81] It has already been seen that, *per se,* joining the Communist Party is not an act directed to contempt of the faith or ecclesiastical authority.[82] For an act to work to the detriment of souls it must be such that it draws people away from the Faith or from the practice of Christian morals and thus expose them to the danger of eternal damnation.[83] Ordinarily, joining the Communist Party will not have such an effect. However, it must be recognized that under certain conditions such an

---

[77] Canon 2229, § 3, 1°.

[78] The censure of canon 2335 is simply reserved to the Holy See. In extraordinary circumstances delegation is granted *a iure* by canons 882, 2252, and 2254 for absolution from censures in the internal forum. The Quinquennial Faculties granted to the Ordinaries of the United States contain the faculty to absolve in either forum from the censures and ecclesiastical penalties incurred by those who have joined the Masons or similar societies. Certain conditions must be fulfilled, however.—*Digest,* Annual Supplement Through 1956, under canon 66.

[79] Canon 2237, § 2.

[80] Canon 2229, § 3, 1°. It is also to be noted that the Decree of the Holy Office on membership in the Party says that the sacraments are to be denied those who "knowingly and freely" join the Party. Cf. *supra,* p. 102.

[81] Canons 2205, § 3; 2229, § 3, 3°; cf. also the response of the Commission for the Authentic Interpretation of the Code, issued in 1937, *Digest,* II, 570-571.

[82] Cf. *supra,* pp. 110-111.

[83] McCoy, *Force and Fear in Relation to Delictual Imputability and Penal Responsibility,* p. 97.

effect is quite possible. Accordingly, if this be the case, then grave fear, necessity or *incommodum* will not excuse from the censure. The same will be true if a given Communist Party is an atheistic sect in the sense of the response given in 1934.[84] Joining such a Party will be an act that is directed to contempt of the faith and hence grave fear, necessity or *incommodum* cannot be offered as excusing causes.

Assuming the penitent demonstrates that he has not incurred the penalty because of the presence of one or more of the excusing causes recognized by law,[85] then the confessor may absolve from the sin,[86] providing the proper dispositions are present.[87] Included in the firm purpose of amendment must be the intention to sever all relations with the Communist Party. Naturally, if the penitent refuses to do this, absolution cannot be granted.[88] The question of passive membership will be treated shortly.[89]

Once the penitent has received absolution, he may resume his normal Christian life. His position is analogous to the situation described in canon 2251. According to this canon, if the absolution of a censure is given in the internal forum only, although this has no legal effect in the external forum, the person thus absolved may conduct himself as one absolved even in regard to acts of the external forum, provided no scandal ensues. Moreover, unless the grant of absolution is proved, or at least susceptible to legitimate presumption, the observance of the censure in the external forum may be demanded by the superiors of the external forum and the delinquent must submit until absolution has been received also

---

[84] Cf. *supra*, pp. 120-121.

[85] E.g., canon 2229 and canon 2205.

[86] Canon 2246, § 3: ". . . verum si quis a censura excusatur vel ab eadem fuit absolutus, reservatio peccati penitus cessant."

[87] Canon 870.

[88] When asked whether or not it was lawful to grant absolution to a Mason who, although he repented of his Masonic oath, nevertheless still communicated with his lodge and frequented its meetings, the Holy Office, on July 5, 1837, replied, *"non licere."*—*Fontes,* IV, n. 877. A year later the Holy Office further declared that such an absolution would be invalid. —*Loc. cit.*

[89] Cf. *infra.*

in the external forum. It must be recalled that once the law is externally violated, *dolus* is presumed until the contrary is proven.[90] Hence, since the absolution from the censure was given only in the internal forum, or in the case at hand, the excusing causes have only been demonstrated in the internal forum, the *dolus* remains presumed in the external forum. However, it can be said that, normally, once the person resumes his Christian life, e.g., participation in the sacraments, he overcomes the presumption.

It has just been said that generally speaking those who join the Communist Party must completely withdraw from the organization before they can be reconciled to the Church.[91] However, according to the Decree of the Holy Office issued in 1949, it would seem that passive membership may be tolerated in certain circumstances. The Decree directs that sacraments are to be refused those who *knowingly* or *freely* join the Communist Party.[92] The commentary given in *L'Osservatore Romano* on the Decree, when treating of the obligation to refuse the sacraments to those who knowingly and freely associate themselves with the Communist cause, says: "Those who wish to remain members of the Communist movement . . . cannot ask to be admitted to the sacraments."[93] However, the commentary then adds:

> But she [the Church] knows full well that there are some of the faithful who, against their own will, by moral and sometimes even by physical force, are compelled to enroll themselves in a Communist Party. In such a case, the priest must be the judge of the circumstances under which the penitent has been compelled to accept the card of a party which he abhors and condemns in his own heart.[94]

Although the Decree of the Holy Office, and the latter quotation from the commentary, speak only of the initial act of joining the

---

[90] Canon 2200, § 2.

[91] Cf. *supra*, p. 163.

[92] Cf. *supra*, p. 102.

[93] *L'Osservatore Romano* 27 July, 1949; translation from *The Tablet*, 194 (1949), n. 5698, p. 87.

[94] *Loc. cit.*

Party, it is obvious that continued membership must be understood. Just as a really serious cause may justify merely material cooperation in the first instance, so also it may—so long as the serious cause remains—justify a failure to end that cooperation. Hence, if a person ran a serious risk of grave harm by handing in his membership card he could be excused from the obligation to do so as long as the serious danger remained.[95] However, the greatest caution must be exercised in granting such permission and scandal must always be removed. Certainly in countries behind the Iron Curtain scandal might not be caused by passive membership, since the faithful are all too familiar with the methods employed by the Communists to "recruit" members to the Party and workers' unions.[96]

Section VI. Matrimony

The special *Declaratio* of the Holy Office regarding the marriages of Communists directs that the marriages of the faithful with those of the faithful who have joined the Communist Party are to be governed by canon 1065 and canon 1066.[97] Both of these canons deal with the marriages of unworthy Catholics.

---

[95] There have been occasions in the past when the Holy See permitted passive membership in condemned societies. For example, the Bishop of St. Hycinth in Canada asked if those persons could be admitted to the sacraments who joined a secret sect to avoid temporal loss. The Holy Office, in 1883, replied: "Iuxta exposita catholicos, de quibus agitur, admitti posse ad sacramenta, praevia absolutione a censuris, quatenus opus sit (pro qua dantur Episcopo opportunae facultates) dummodo: 1. reapse sese omnino separaverint a societatibus praedictis;—2. promittant numquam amplius fore ut sese immisceant alicui actui societatum ipsarum tum secreto tum publico, et praesertim numquam amplius se soluturos requisitam contributionem;—3. removeatur scandalum eo meliori modo quo fieri potest;—4. animo sint dispositi ad suum nomen revocandum, si et quando id facere absque gravi damno poterunt."—*Fontes,* IV, n. 1080. Cf. also Beste, *Introductio in Codicem* (4. ed.), pp. 1038, 1041.

[96] In many countries behind the Iron Curtain refusal to join the Party or Communist organizations is punishable by death, imprisonment or loss of employment.—Conway, "The Decree of the Holy Office on Communism," *The Irish Ecclesiastical Record,* LXXIII (1950), 62.

[97] Cf. *supra,* p. 60.

It should be noted that canon 1065 requires that the person's enrollment in the condemned society be notorious.[98] It the person's membership lacks the notion of notoriety, as long as it constitutes him a public sinner, then he will fall under the group known as public sinners, and therefore he will be subject to the prescriptions of canon 1066.[99] The term "public sinner" used in canon 1066 includes the persons mentioned in canon 1065, as well as those who have committed public sins which are not actually delicts.[100]

Canon 1065, § 2 and canon 1066 require the presence of a grave cause before the priest may assist at the marriages of the faithful with publicly unworthy Catholics. Causes which are considered sufficient to justify the granting of a dispensation from the impediments of mixed religion or disparity of cult are likewise sufficient to warrant the cessation of the prohibition of canons 1065, and 1066. However, since these canons do not constitute a canonical impediment, other causes which are not considered as canonical for a dispensation from matrimonial impediments may be urged for these marriages.[101] Both canons require the permission of the Ordinary.

Canon 1065, § 2 demands moral certainty regarding the Catholic education of the offspring and the removal of the danger of perversion of the other party. Since the dangers present in mixed marriages are also present in the marriages referred to in canons 1065 and 1066, though perhaps in a given case they are not as proximate, the same conditions must be verified. Heneghan, following the majority of canonists, holds that the formal promises are not strictly required for these cases.[102] However, they might

---

[98] "Absterreantur quoque fideles a matrimonio contrahendo cum iis qui notorie . . . societatibus ab Ecclesia damnatis adscripti sunt."

[99] "Si publicus peccator . . . prius ad sacramentalem confessionem accedere aut cum Ecclesia reconciliari recusaverit, parochus eius matrimonio ne assistat, nisi gravis urgeat causa, de qua, si fieri possit, consulat Ordinarium."

[100] Heneghan, *The Marriages of Unworthy Catholics, Canons 1065 and 1066,* The Catholic University of America Canon Law Studies, n. 188. (Washington, D. C.: The Catholic University of America Press, 1944), p. 113.

[101] *Ibid.,* pp. 158-159.

[102] *Op. cit.,* p. 167.

be determined by particular law. Heneghan also notes that in the marriages of publicly unworthy Catholics the banns must be publicly announced.[103] However, for a just reason they may be dispensed. Ordinarily, these marriages should be celebrated as the marriages of two Catholics in the parish church in accordance with the rule of canon 1109, § 1. However, as Quigley observes, if the local Ordinary foresees that grave scandal will arise from the celebration of such marriages in the church itself, he may forbid the use of the church for this purpose and may grant permission for the marriage to be celebrated outside of church and in a decent place.[104]

Heneghan says that the local Ordinary may permit as a general rule the use of the sacred rites which are ordinarily obligatory in the celebration of Catholic marriages, excluding only the Nuptial Mass and Solemn Blessing.[105] However, it should be noted that the Decree of the Holy Office concerning the marriages of Communists refers to canon 1102, the canon which regulates the sacred rites to be used in mixed marriages, only in connection with the marriages of those who profess Communism.[106] Hence, the Nuptial Mass and Solemn Blessing may be permitted in the marriages of those who merely join the Party. In practice, however, the matter must be left to the judgment of the Ordinary.

Section VII. Infamia Facti

Finally, if in the judgment of the local Ordinary one who has joined the Communist Party has become infamous (*infamia facti*),[107] then the person will be subject to the limitations placed upon him by canon 2294, § 2. Hence, those who have incurred infamy of fact must be excluded from the reception of orders in accordance with canon 987, 7° ; from the appointment to dignities,

---

[103] *Op. cit.*, p. 171.

[104] Quigley, *Condemned Societies*, p. 106.

[105] *Op. cit.*, p. 176

[106] "But in the marriages of the persons referred to in n. 4 of the aforesaid Decree (those who profess Communism), the provisions of canon 1061, 1102, and 1109, § 3 are to be observed."—*AAS*, XXXXI (1949), 427; *Digest*, III, 407-408; cf. *supra*, p. 60, for text. Cf. also *supra*, pp. 120, 121.

[107] Canon 2293, § 3.

benefices, and offices; from the exercise of the sacred ministry; and from legitimate ecclesiastical acts such as sponsorship at baptism and confirmation.[108]

ARTICLE 3. THOSE WHO FAVOR THE COMMUNIST MOVEMENT

Since the notion of favoring the Communist movement, as well as the canonico-juridical status of *fautores,* has already been discussed in the previous chapter,[109] the present article confines itself to a brief examination of some of the legal effects incurred by this group of Communists.

At the outset it is necessary to recall that the term "favoring" is a broad term, embracing a wide variety of acts. It even includes propagating and defending a movement. For that reason, it is well to recall here that if the acts a person performs in behalf of the Communist movement are such that they create a violent suspicion that he is professing Communism, then the person is to be considered an apostate and therefore he falls under the provisions of canon 2314. Moreover, if a person performs certain acts which assist in the propagation of Communist doctrines, under certain conditions he may be rendered suspect of heresy.[110] In that event the person must be warned by the proper authority to remove the causes of suspicion.[111] If this admonition proves fruitless, the suspected person must be forbidden to perform legal ecclesiastical acts, according to canon 2265. If he is a cleric, he must be suspended *a divinis,* after a second warning has been left unheeded. If within six months thereafter he has not removed the suspicion, he must be regarded as a heretic and subject to the penalties of canon 2314.

However, it is very possible that a person's acts performed in behalf of Communism, will create no suspicion at all concerning the state of his mind in heresy,[112] even if these acts are public

[108] Canon 2294, § 2. It must be remembered that one who has joined the Party is subject to the various effects of excommunication listed in the previous article—cf. *supra,* pp. 146-156.

[109] Cf. *supra,* pp. 121-141.

[110] Canon 2316; cf. *supra,* pp. 78-80.

[111] Canon 2315.

[112] Canon 2316.

and in the eyes of the faithful the person is regarded as a public sinner.[113] The present article is concerned with such acts. The other acts mentioned above, that is, those which create suspicions concerning the state of the person's mind, have already been treated in a previous article.[114]

The primary legal effect resulting from *knowingly* and *freely* performing acts in favor of the Communist movement is that the person renders himself unworthy to receive the sacraments since he is not properly disposed.[115] Hence, unless the *fautor* promises to desist from favoring the movement, he cannot receive sacramental absolution.[116] If the individual is publicly known as one who favors the Communist movement, he is to be excluded from the reception of Holy Communion, unless his repentance and amendment are publicly known.[117] The minister shall likewise refuse to admit those whose acts of favoring the Communist movement are occult if the minister knows the person has not repented. But the minister shall not do so if the delinquent publicly requests Holy Communion and the minister is unable to pass him by without scandal.[118]

Regarding the administration of the sacrament of extreme unction to those who have favored the Communist movement, the prescriptions of canon 942 must be followed. Hence, the sacrament shall not be administered to those who contumaciously remain impenitent in manifest mortal sin. But if there is a doubt in this regard, it should be administered conditionally.[119]

If a person, because of the acts which he has performed in behalf of the Communist movement, is a public sinner, then his marriage is to be governed according to the prescriptions of canon

---

[113] Cf. n. 1 of the Decree of the Holy Office on Communism, *supra*, pp. 59-60.

[114] Cf. *supra*, pp. 78-80.

[115] This is stated in n. 1 of the Decree of the Holy Office, cf. *supra*, pp. 59-60.

[116] Canon 870. It is presumed there is no justifying reason to continue the cooperation.

[117] Canon 855.

[118] Canon 855, § 2.

[119] Cf. also canon 943 for administering this sacrament to those destitute of their senses.

1066.[120] This canon has already been briefly treated in the previous article.[121]

Canon 1240, § 1, 6° directs that "other public and manifest sinners" are to be deprived of ecclesiastical burial. It is disputed by the authors whether this canon punishes notorious sinners or only notorious delinquents. In other words, it is not altogether clear whether one may incur the penalty of the privation of Christian burial by the commission of a notorious transgression which is not a delict in the strict sense of canon 2195, § 1. Mere favoring of the Communist movement, in the sense of n. 1 of the Decree of the Holy Office, is not a delict.

Kerin, treating the question of public sinners, says that, because of the doubt whether all public sinners are also public delinquents, the strict sense of public delinquents in the sense of canon 2195 should be retained since there is a penalty involved.[122] As was noted above, one who merely favors Communism does not *per se* become a public delinquent. However, Kerin adds that the difficulty in regard to the notion of public sinners is largely speculative. Even were one not guilty of a notorious delict in the sense of canon 2195, § 1, the notoriety of his sin, presuming it were notorious, would deprive him of Christian burial because of the very probable danger of grave scandal in its concession to one so publicly unworthy.[123] It is inconceivable, he says, that a Christian burial of one who is notoriously a public sinner would not cause grave scandal.[124] These conclusions concerning Christian burial are certainly applicable to a person who is a public and manifest (notorious) sinner because of the acts which he has performed in behalf of the Communist movement.

---

[120] This is the regulation set down by the *Declaratio* of the Holy Office regarding marriage with those who favor Communism, cf. *supra*, p. 60. It is necessary to recall that a person need not be a member of the Party in order to show favor to the Communist movement, cf. *supra*, pp. 38-40.

[121] Cf. *supra*, pp. 165-167.

[122] *The Privation of Christian Burial*, p. 223. The deprivation of Christian burial is generally looked upon as a penalty, *ibid.*, p. 131.

[123] *Op. cit.*, p. 223.

[124] *Loc. cit.* Cf. canon 2197, 3° for definition of notorious; cf. also *supra*, p. 156.

It should also be noted that those persons, who are considered public sinners because of their acts performed in behalf of the Communist movement, if in the judgment of the local Ordinary they have become infamous (*infamia facti*),[125] will be subject to the restrictions placed upon them by canon 2294, § 2. Therefore, they will be excluded from the reception of orders in accordance with canon 987, 7° ; from the appointment of dignities, benefices, and offices, from the exercise of the sacred ministry and from legitimate acts. The last restriction will include sponsorship and baptism and confirmation.[126]

---

[125] Canon 2293, § 3.
[126] Canons 766 and 796.

CONCLUSIONS

1. The term "Communist" should be understood as embracing three categories of people: those who profess Communism, those who join the Communist Party, and those who show favor to the movement (pp. vii, 71).
2. Since the basic principle of Communist tactics is adaptability, the Party operates differently in each country. Hence, in deciding the canonico-juridical status of a person who associates himself with the movement, consideration must always be given to the circumstances of time and place (pp. 20-33).
3. The term "Communist Parties" employed in the Decrees of the Holy Office on Communism must be understood as including Communist Fronts, since these organizations are under the control of the Party, and each one in its own way is fighting the Party's battles (pp. 34-40).
4. The authors who uphold the opinion that a sect must be secret in order to be similar to the Masons fail to offer valid proofs to substantiate their claim. Neither the historical background of canon 2335, nor the wording of the canon indicates that secrecy is an essential feature in the phrase *"eiusdem generis."* Moreover, it is incorrect to claim that the Decree of the Holy Office issued in 1949, on the question of association with the Communists, upholds the opinion that secrecy is an essential feature in those sects which are condemned under censure in canon 2335 (pp. 87-108).
5. Since the Communist Party is a sect similar to the Masons, those who join the Communist Party incur the same penalty as those who join the Masons—an excommunication simply reserved to the Holy See (pp. 99-108).
6. The precise crime punished in canon 2335 is the initial overt act placed by a person, be it by writing, word, or deed, which is accepted by the organization as signifying membership. Therefore, if one joins the Communist Party (or a Communist

Front) in good faith and subsequently learns that joining said group is forbidden under censure, but refuses to separate, he does not then incur the censure of canon 2335. However, he must be refused the sacraments (pp. 108, 113-114).

7. When complete separation from the Communist Party would result in grave harm to the individual, passive membership may be tolerated, *remoto scandalo* (pp. 164-165).
8. A society, even though one of its chief tenets is the denial of God, cannot be considered a true and *proprie dicta* atheistic sect according to the sense of the response given by the Pontifical Commission for the Authentic Interpretation of the Code of Canon Law in 1934, unless the organization professes atheism as its particular, primary and proper end. Moreover, atheism must be the principal source and foundation of the organization's doctrinal system, the fountainhead of its other doctrinal errors, norms of living and acting. Since the Communist Party, *ut sic,* does not fulfill these conditions, it cannot be considered the type of atheistic sect envisioned by the response of 1934 (pp. 116-121).
9. Those who persist in showing favor to the Communist movement must be refused the sacraments. If a person assists in the propagation of Communistic doctrines, and his cooperation creates a vehement suspicion concerning the state of his mind in heresy, then according to canon 2316 he is suspect of heresy. If the acts which a person performs in behalf of the Communist movement are such that they create a violent suspicion that he is professing Communism, then he will fall under the provisions of canon 2314 as an apostate (pp. 78-80, 127).
10. The traditional meaning assigned to the term "favor" by the authors can be of service in understanding the term as it is used in the Decree of the Holy Office of 1949 on association with or participation in the Communist movement. The term includes those who negatively assist the movement, that is, those in official positions who are obliged in virtue of their office to hinder the spread of Communism and fail to do so. The term also includes those who favor the movement by assisting it in a positive way (pp. 124-126).

11. The marriages of the faithful with those of the faithful who profess Communism are not mixed marriages, and therefore a dispensation *mixtae religionis* is not required. But such marriages must be treated like mixed marriages, and hence the prescriptions of canon 1061, 1102, and 1109, § 3, must be followed (pp. 151-154).

BIBLIOGRAPHY

Sources

Acta Apostolicae Sedis, Commentarium Officiale, Romae, 1909-1929; Civitate Vaticana, 1929-

Acta et Decreta Concilii Plenarii Baltimorensis Tertii (1884), Baltimore: John Murphy, 1886.

Acta Sanctae Sedis, 41 vols., Romae, 1865-1908.

Bouscaren, T. Lincoln, *The Canon Law Digest,* 3 vols. and Supplements through 1956, Milwaukee: Bruce & Co., 1934-1949-1953-1954-1955-1956.

Codex Iuris Canonici, Pii X Pontificis Maximi iussu digestus Benedicti Papae XV auctoritate promulgatus, Praefatione, Fontium Annotatione et Indice Analytico-Alphebetico ab Eñio Petri Card. Gasparri Auctus, Romae: Typis Polyglottis Vaticanis, 1917; reimpressio, 1946.

Codicis Iuris Canonici Fontes, cura Eñi Petri Card. Gasparri, editi, 9 vols., Romae (postea Civitate Vaticana): Typis Polyglottis Vaticanis, 1923-1939 (Vols. VII-IX, ed. cura et studio Eñi. Iustiniani Card. Serédi).

Communism in Action, A Documented Study and Analysis of Communism in Operation in the Soviet Union, Prepared at the instance and under the direction of Representative Everett M. Dirksen of Illinois, by the Legislative Reference Service of The Library of Congress, 79th Congress, 2nd Session, House Document No. 754, United States Government Printing Office, 1946.

Concilii Plenarii Baltimorensis II, in Ecclesia Metropolitana Baltimorensi, a die VII, ad diem XXI Octobris, A. D. 1866 Habiti et a Sede Apostolica Recogniti Acta et Decreta, Baltimorae: Joannes Murphy, 1868.

Magnum Bullarium Romanum, 19 vols. in 18, Luxemburgi, 1727-1754.

Organized Communism in the United States, a pamphlet prepared and released by the Committee on Un-American Activities, United States House of Representatives, Washington, D. C., United States Government Printing Office, 1953.

The Communist Party of the United States of America, a pamphlet prepared by the Subcommittee on Internal Security of the Senate Committee on the Judiciary, 84th Congress, 2nd Session, Senate Document No. 117, United States Government Printing Office, 1956.

The Great Encyclical Letters of Pope Leo XIII, New York: Benziger Brothers, 1903.

The Great Pretense, A Symposium on Anti-Stalinism and the 20th Congress of the Soviet Communist Party, a pamphlet prepared and released by the Committee on Un-American Activities, United States House of

Representatives, Washington, D. C., 84th Congress, 2nd Session, House Report No. 2189, United States Government Printing Office, 1956.

Reference Works

Abbo, John-Hannan, Jerome, *The Sacred Canons,* 2 vols., St. Louis: B. Herder Book Co., 1952.

Aertnys, Josephus, *Theologia Moralis Iuxta Doctrinam S. Alphonsi de Ligorio,* 2 vols., Tornaci, 1893.

Almond, Gabriel, *Appeals of Communism,* Princeton: Princeton University Press, 1954.

Alterius, Marcus, *Disputationes De Censuris Ecclesiasticis,* 2 vols., Romae, 1616.

Augustine, Charles, *A Commentary on Canon Law,* 8 vols., Vol. VIII, 3. ed., St. Louis: B. Herder Book Co., 1931.

Ayrinhac, H., *Administrative Legislation in the New Code of Canon Law,* New York: Longmans, Green & Co., 1930.

Ayrinhac, H.-Lydon, P., *Penal Legislation in the New Code of Canon Law,* New York: Benziger Brothers, 1936.

Ballerini, Antonius, *Opus Theologicum Morale,* absolvit et editit Dominicus Palmieri, 7 vols., Prati, 1889-1893.

Bargilliat, Michael, *Praelectiones Iuris Canonici,* 28. ed., 2 vols., Parisiis: Berche et Tralin, Editores, 1913.

Beste, U., *Introductio in Codicem,* 4. ed., Neapoli: D'Auria Pontificius Editor, 1956.

Blat, Albertus, *Commentarium Textus Iuris Canonici,* 5 vols. in 6, Romae: Ex Typographia Pontificia in Instituto Pii X, Vol. V, 1. ed., 1924.

Bouscaren, T. L.-Ellis, A. C., *Canon Law, A Text and Commentary,* 3. ed., rev., Milwaukee: The Bruce Publishing Co., 1957.

Bucceroni, Ianuarius, *Institutiones Theologiae Moralis,* 6. ed., 4 vols., Romae, 1915.

Budenz, Louis, *The Techniques of Communism,* Chicago: Henry Regnery Co., 1954.

Cappello, Felix, *De Censuris Iuxta Codicem Iuris Canonici,* 3. ed., 1933; 4. ed., 1950, Taurinorum Augustae: Marietti.

Chamberlin, William, *Blueprint for World Conquest,* Washington, D. C.: Human Events, 1946.

Chelodi, Ioannes, *Ius Poenale et Ordo Procedendi in Iudiciis Criminalibus,* Tridenti: Libr. Edit. Tridentum, 1925.

Cianfarra, Camille, *The Vatican and the Kremlin,* New York: E. P. Dutton & Co., 1950.

Cima, *Commentario alla Costituzione Apostolicae Sedis,* Genova, 1890.

Cipollini, Albertus, *De Censuris Latae Sententiae Iuxta Codicem Iuris Canonici,* Taurini: Marietti, 1925.

Conte a Coronata, Matthaeus, *Institutiones Iuris Canonici,* 5 vols., Vol. I-

III, 2. ed., 1939-1941; Vol. IV, 4. ed., 1955; Vol. V, 3. ed., 1951; Taurini-Romae: Marietti.

D'Annibale, Iosephus, *Summula Theologiae Moralis,* 3. ed., 3 vols., Romae: 1891-1892.

De Luca, M., *Liber de Delictis et Poenis Ecclesiasticis,* Romae, 1901.

Eichmann, Eduard, *Das Strafrecht des Codex Iuris Canonici,* Paderborn: Schöningh, 1920.

Elbel, Beniaminus, *Theologia Moralis Per Modum Conferentiarum,* ed., Irenaeus Bierbaum, 3 vols., Paderbornae, 1892.

Farrugia, Nicolaus, *Commentarium in Censuris Latae Sententiae Codicis Iuris Canonici,* 2. ed., Melitae, 1921.

Fisher, Marguerite, *Communist Doctrine and the Free World,* Syracuse: Syracuse University Press, 1952.

Galter, Albert, *The Red Book of the Persecuted Church,* Westminster, Md.: The Newman Press, 1957.

Genicot, Eduardus, *Institutiones Theologiae Moralis,* 2 vols., Lovanii, 1896; 6. ed., recognita et aucta a J. Salamans, Bruxellis, 1909.

Gurian, Waldemar, *Bolshevism,* Notre Dame: University of Notre Dame Press, 1952.

Hales, Edward, *Pio Nono,* New York: P. J. Kenedy, 1954.

Halecki, Oscar-Murray, James, *Pius XII: Eugenio Pacelli, Pope of Peace,* Farrar, Straus and Young, Inc., 1951.

Hayes, Carlton, J., *A Political and Social History of Modern Europe,* 1. ed., 2 vols., New York: Macmillan Co., 1918.

Heneghan, John, *The Marriages of Unworthy Catholics, Canons 1065 and 1066,* The Catholic University of America Canon Law Studies, n. 188, Washington, D. C.: The Catholic University of America Press, 1944.

Hoover, J. Edgar, *Masters of Deceit,* New York: Henry Holt & Co., 1958.

Husslein, J., *Social Wellsprings,* 2 vols., Milwaukee: Bruce Publishing Co., 1943.

Hyland, Francis E., *Excommunication, Its Nature, Historical Development and Effects,* The Catholic University of America Canon Law Studies, n. 49, Washington, D. C.: The Catholic University of America, 1928.

Kerin, Charles A., *The Privation of Christian Burial,* The Catholic University of America Canon Law Studies, n. 136, Washington, D. C.: The Catholic University of America Press, 1941.

Kilker, Adrian J., *Extreme Unction,* The Catholic University of America Canon Law Studies, n. 32, Washington, D. C.: The Catholic University of America, 1926.

Know Your Communist Enemy, a series of pamphlets published by the Office of Armed Forces Information and Education, Department of Defense, Washington, D. C., n. 1, *International Communism: Its Aims and Methods,* 1954; n. 4, *In the Iron Grip of the Kremlin,* 1955, United States Government Printing Office.

Laymann, Paulus, *Theologia Moralis,* 2 vols. in 1, Venetiis, 1630.

Lega, Michael, *Praelectiones in Textum Iuris Canonici,* 2. ed., 4 vols., Romae, 1905.

Lehmkuhl, Augustinus, *Theologia Moralis,* 12. ed., 2 vols., Friburgi Brisgoviae, 1914.

Lenin, Nikolai, *Left Wing Communism,* New York: International Publishers, 1934.

———, *Religion,* New York: International Publishers, 1933.

———, *What Is To Be Done?* New York: International Publishers, 1929.

Lerhinan, John P., *A Sociological Commentary on "Divini Redemptoris,"* The Catholic University of America, Washington, D. C.: The Catholic University of America Press, 1946.

MacDonald, Fergus, *The Catholic Church and Secret Societies in the United States,* ed. T. McMahon, New York: The United States Catholic Historical Society, Monograph Series XXII, 1946.

McFadden, Charles J., *The Philosophy of Communism,* New York: Benziger Bros., 1939.

MacKenzie, Eric F., *The Delict of Heresy in Its Commission, Penalization, Absolution,* The Catholic University of America Canon Law Studies, n. 77, Washington, D. C.: The Catholic University of America, 1932.

Marx, Karl, *Communist Manifesto,* Chicago: Henry Regnery Co., 1949.

McCoy, Alan E., *Force and Fear in Relation to Delictual Imputability and Penal Responsibility,* The Catholic University of America Canon Law Studies, n. 200, Washington, D. C.: The Catholic University of America Press, 1944.

Michel, A., *Dividing the Church,* London: Sword of the Spirit, 1956.

Nilles, N., *Commentaria in Concilium Plenarium Baltimorense Tertium,* 2 vols., Oeniponte, Ex Officina F. Rauch (C. Pustet), 1888.

Noldin, H., *De Poenis Ecclesiasticis,* 5. ed., Oeniponte, 1905.

Noldin, H.-Schmitt, A., *Summa Theologiae Moralis,* 3 vols., Vol. II, 27. ed., Oeniponte: Typis et Sumptibus Fel. Rauch, 1941.

Ottaviani, Alaphridus, *Institutiones Iuris Publici Ecclesiastici,* 2 vols., Romae: Typis Polyglottis Vaticanis, Vol. I, 3. ed., 1947; Vol. II, 2. ed., 1936.

Palazzini, P., *Casus Conscientiae,* 3 vols., Vol. II, *De Censuris,* Romae: Officium Libri Catholici, 1956.

Pelle, P., *Le Droit Pénal De L'Église,* Paris: P. Lethielleux, Libraire-Éditeur, 1939.

Pernicone, Joseph M., *The Ecclesiastical Prohibition of Books,* The Catholic University of America Canon Law Studies, n. 72, Washington, D. C.: The Catholic University of America, 1932.

Piatus Montensis, *Commentarium in Constitutionem Apostolicae Sedis,* Tornaci, 1881.

Pighi, J., *Censurae Latae Sententiae et Irregularitates,* 5. ed., Veronae, 1919.

Pirhing, Ernricus, *Ius Canonicum Nova Methodo Explicatum,* 5 vols. in 4, Dilingae, 1674-1678.

Pistocchi, Mario, *I Canoni Penali del Codice Ecclesiastico Espositi e Commentati,* Torino-Roma: Marietti, 1925.

Prümmer, Dominicus M., *Manuale Theologiae Moralis,* 3. ed., 3 vols., Friburgi Brisgoviae, 1923.

Quigley, Joseph A., *Condemned Societies,* The Catholic University of America Canon Law Studies, n. 46, Washington, D. C.: The Catholic University of America, 1927.

Regatillo, Eduardus F., *Institutiones Iuris Canonici,* 4. ed., 2 vols., Santander: Sal Terrae, 1951.

Reiffenstuel, Anacletus, *Jus Canonicum Universum,* 7 vols., Parisiis, 1864-1870.

Rodimer, Frank J., *The Canonical Effects of Infamy of Fact,* The Catholic University of America Canon Law Studies, n. 353, Washington, D. C.: The Catholic University of America Press, 1954.

Sabetti, A., *Compendium Theologiae Moralis,* 12. ed., Neo Eboraci et Cincinnati, 1896.

Salucci, Raffaele, *Il Diritto Penale Secondo il Codice di Diritto Canonico,* 2 vols. in 1, Subiaco: Tipografia dei Monasteri, 1926-1930.

Salvadori, M., *The Rise of Communism,* New York: Henry Holt & Co., 1952.

Sanchez, T., *Opus Morale in Praecepto Decalogi,* 2 vols., Parmae, 1723.

Schmalzgrueber, Franciscus, *Ius Ecclesiasticum Universum,* 5 vols. in 12, Romae, 1843-1845.

Schaefer, Timotheus, *De Religiosis ad Normam Codicis Iuris Canonici,* 3. ed., Romae: Typis Polyglottis Vaticanis, 1940.

Sole, Iacobus, *De Delictis et Poenis,* Romae: Pustet, 1920.

Stalin, Joseph, *History of the Communist Party of the Soviet Union (Bolshevik),* New York: International Publishers, 1939.

———, *Leninism,* 2 vols., New York: International Publishers (no date of publication).

Suarez, Franciscus, *Opera Omnia,* Vivès editio, ed. Carolus Berton, 26 vols., Parisiis, 1856-1861, Vol. XXIII, *De Censuris,* 1861.

Swoboda, Innocent, *Ignorance in Relation to the Imputability of Delicts,* The Catholic University of America Canon Law Studies, n. 143, Washington, D. C.: The Catholic University of America Press, 1941.

Tanquerey, A., *Synopsis Theologiae Moralis et Pastoralis,* 7. ed., 3 vols., Romae, 1922.

Tatarczuk, Vincent A., *Infamy of Law,* The Catholic University of America Canon Law Studies, n. 357, Washington, D. C.: The Catholic University of America Press, 1954.

Teeling, William, *Pope Pius XI and World Affairs,* New York: F. Stokes Co., 1937.

Thomas Aquinas, St., *Summa Theologica,* 5 vols., Taurini: Marietti, 1938.

Vermeersch, A., *De Prohibitione et Censura Librorum,* 2. ed., Romae, 1898.

Vermeersch, A.-Creusen, J., *Epitome Iuris Canonici,* 3 vols., Vol. I, 7. ed.,

1949; Vol. II, 6. ed., 1940; Vol. III, 6. ed., 1946, Mechlinae-Romae: H. Dessain.

Vogelpohl, Henry J., *The Simple Impediments to Holy Orders,* The Catholic University of America Canon Law Studies, n. 224, Washington, D. C.: The Catholic University of America Press, 1945.

Walsh, Edmund A., *Why Pope Pius XI Asked Prayers for Russia on March 19, 1930,* pamphlet published by The Catholic Near East Welfare Association, New York, 1930.

Wernz, F., *Ius Decretalium,* 6 vols., Vols. I-IV, 2. ed., 1905-1912; Vols. V-VI, 1913-1914, Romae.

———, Vidal, P., *Ius Canonicum ad Codicis Normam Exactum,* 7 vols. in 8, Romae: Universitatas Gregoriana, 1923-1938.

Woywod, S., *A Practical Commentary on the Code of Canon Law,* 2 vols., New York: Joseph F. Wagner, Inc., 1925.

Zitelli, Zephyrinus, *Apparatus Iuris Ecclesiastici,* 3. ed., Romae, 1903.

Zubek, Theodoric, *The Church of Silence in Slovakia,* Whiting: J. J. Lach, 1956.

Articles

Anon.—"Il Decreto Sul Comunismo," *L'Osservatore Romano,* July 27, 1949.

Anon.—"The Decree of the Holy Office Against Communism" (translation of the commentary, "Il Decreto Sul Comunismo," *L'Osservatore Romano,* July 27, 1949), *The Tablet,* August 6, 1949, p. 87.

Bidagor, P., "Adnotationes," *Monitor Ecclesiasticus,* LXXIV (1949), 49-55.

Cardini, Aloysius, "Adnotationes," *Monitor Ecclesiasticus,* LXXV (1950), 545-548.

Ciprotti, Pio, "De Consummatione Delicti," *Apollinaris,* VIII (1935), 224-248.

Claeys Boúúaert, F., "De Metus Influxu quoad Valorem Actuum et quoad Delicta et Poenas Secundum Codicem Iuris Canonici," *Jus Pontificium,* VI (1926), 105-111; 138-144.

Conway, William, "The Decree of the Holy Office on Communism," *The Irish Ecclesiastical Record,* 5. series, LXXIII (1950), 58-65.

Fabregas, Michael, "Annotationes," *Periodica,* XXXIX (1950), 310-314.

Fagiolo, "Consulationes," *Monitor Ecclesiasticus,* LXXV (1950), 480.

Ganzi, Hyginus, "Nomen Dantes Communismo," *Periodica,* XXXVII (1947), 103-118.

Hook, Sidney, "The Fellow Traveler: A Study in Psychology," *The New York Times Magazine,* April 17, 1949, pp. 9, 20-23.

Jombart, E., "Annotationes," *Nouvelle Revue Théologique,* LXI (1934), 1076-1078.

Katzer, Frederick X., "Societies Forbidden in the Church," *The American Ecclesiastical Review,* VI (1892), 241-247.

Maroto, Philippus, "Annotationes super Responsis Die 30 Iulii 1934 Datis a Pontif. Commissione ad Codicis Canones authentice Interpretandos," *Commentarium pro Religiosis et Missionariis,* XV (1935), 337-346.

McReavy, Lawrence L., "The Holy Office on Communism," *The Clergy Review,* XXXII (1949), 389-398.

Ottaviani, Alaphridus, "De Communistarum Matrimoniis," *Apollinaris,* XXII (1949), 101-105.

Poglajen, F., "Les Differéntes Organisations Athées," *Nouvelle Revue Théologique,* LXI (1934), 1069-1073.

Sirna, Iosephus, "Adnotationes ad Decretum S. Officii de Communismo," *Apollinaris,* XXII (1949), 56-70.

Woywod, Stanislaus, "Joining the Freemasons and Similar Societies," *Homiletic and Pastoral Review,* XXXVI (1937), 1281-1285.

Zubek, Theodoric, "Dissolving of the Church Organization in the Countries behind the 'Iron Curtain,'" *Homiletic and Pastoral Review,* LV (1955), 107-116.

———, "The Latest Communistic Tactics in Fighting the Church," *Homiletic and Pastoral Review,* LIV (1954), 301-305; 405-414.

PERIODICALS

American Ecclesiastical Review, The, Vols. I-XXXII, Philadelphia, 1889-1905; *The Ecclesiastical Review,* Vols. XXXIII-CIX, Philadelphia, 1905-1943; *The American Ecclesiastical Review,* Vol. CX-, Washington, D. C., 1944-

Apollinaris, Romae, 1928-

Clergy Review, The, London, 1931-

Commentarium pro Religiosis, Romae, 1920-1934; *Commentarium pro Religiosis et Missionariis,* Romae, 1935-

Homiletical and Pastoral Review, The, New York, 1900-

Irish Ecclesiastical Record, The, Dublin, 1864-; 5th Series, 1913-

Jus Pontificium, Romae, 1921-1940.

Monitore Ecclesiastico, Il, 1876-1948; *Monitor Ecclesiasticus,* Romae, 1949-

New York Times, The, New York, 1851-

Nouvelle Revue Théologique, Paris, 1869-

Osservatore Romano, Città del Vaticano, September 5, 1849-May 27, 1852; July 1, 1861-

Periodica de Religiosis et Missionariis, Brugis, 1905-1919; *Periodica de Re Canonica et Morali, utilia praesertim Religiosis et Missionariis,* Brugis, 1920-1927; *Periodica de Re Morali, Canonica, Liturgica,* Brugis, 1927-1936, Romae, 1937-

Tablet, The, London, 1840-

ABBREVIATIONS

AAS—*Acta Apostolicae Sedis.*

ASS—*Acta Sanctae Sedis.*

De Censuris—Cappello, *De Censuris iuxta Codicem Iuris Canonici.*

Digest—*The Canon Law Digest.*

Institutiones—Conte a Coronata, *Institutiones Iuris Canonici.*

MacKenzie—*The Delict of Heresy in Its Commission, Penalization, Absolution.*

Periodica—*Periodica de Re Canonica, Morali, Liturgica.*

BIOGRAPHICAL NOTE

Richard J. Murphy was born in Brooklyn, New York, on May 17, 1925. He received his elementary education at St. Edmund's parochial school in Brooklyn. In 1939 he entered Brooklyn Preparatory School and was graduated in 1943. In 1946 he enrolled in Boston College, Boston, Massachusetts. The following year he entered Our Lady of Hope Mission Seminary, Newburgh, New York, and in 1948 was admitted to the novitiate of the Oblates of Mary Immaculate at Ipswich, Massachusetts. His philosophical and theological courses were received at the Oblate College, Washington, D. C. He was ordained to the priesthood on May 30, 1954. The following year he received the degree of Licentiate in Sacred Theology from the Catholic University of America. In the same year he enrolled in the School of Canon Law of the Catholic University of America, and received the Baccalaureate degree in Canon Law in June of 1956, and the degree of Licentiate in Canon Law in June of 1957.

ALPHABETICAL INDEX

CANON LAW STUDIES*

392. ADAMS, REV. DONALD E., A.B., J.C.L., The truth required in the *preces* for rescripts.
393. BÉGIN, REV. RAYMOND F., A.B., S.T.L., J.C.L., Natural law and positive law.
394. CLANCY, REV. WALTER B., A.B., J.C.L., The rites and ceremonies of sacred ordination.
395. COX, REV. RONALD J., S.T.L., J.C.L., A study of the juridic status of laymen in the writing of the medieval canonists.
396. DEMERS, REV. FRANCIS L., O.M.I., A.B., J.C.L., Temporal administration of the religious house in a non-exempt clerical pontifical institute.
397. DZIADOSZ, REV. HENRY J., M.A., S.T.L., J.C.L., The provisions of the Decree "Spiritus Sancti munera": the law for the extraordinary minister of confirmation.
398. GERHARDT, REV. BERNARD C., A.B., S.T.L., J.C.L., Interpretation of rescripts.
399. HACKETT, REV. JOHN H., A.B., J.C.L., The concept of public order.
400. MURPHY, REV. RICHARD J., O.M.I., S.T.L., J.C.L., The canonico-juridical status of a communist.
401. O'CONNOR, REV. DAVID, M.S.SS.T., J.C.L., Parochial relations and co-operation of the religious and secular clergy.

*For a complete list of the available numbers of this series apply to the Catholic University of America Press, 620 Michigan Avenue, N.E., Washington (17), D. C., for a general catalogue.

www.ingramcontent.com/pod-product-compliance
Lightning Source LLC
LaVergne TN
LVHW050236080826
844660LV00012B/544

* 9 7 8 0 8 1 3 2 2 5 6 0 9 *